Private Property and the Endangered Species Act

Saving Habitats,

   Protecting Homes

Private Property and the Endangered Species Act

EDITED BY JASON F. SHOGREN

UNIVERSITY OF TEXAS PRESS ⟡ AUSTIN

Portions of this manuscript have appeared previously in *Land and Water Law Review,* vol. 32; *Endangered Species Update,* vol. 14; and *ELR (Environmental Law Reporter) News and Analysis,* vol. 26.

First edition, 1998

Requests for permission to reproduce material from this work should be sent to Permissions, University of Texas Press, Box 7819, Austin, TX 78713-7819.

∞The paper used in this publication meets the minimum requirements of American National Standard for Information Sciences—Permanence of Paper for Printed Library Materials, ANSI Z39.48-1984.

Library of Congress Cataloging-in-Publication Data

Private property and the Endangered Species Act : saving habitats, protecting homes / edited by Jason F. Shogren. — 1st ed.
    p.   cm.
    Includes index.
    ISBN 0-292-77736-1 (cloth) —ISBN 0-292-77737-X (pbk.)
    1.Endangered species—Law and legislation—United States.   2. Wildlife conservation—Law and legislation—United States.   3. Right of property—United States.   I. Shogren, Jason F.
    KF5640 .P75   1998
    346.7304′69522—ddc21   98-9067

To Maija and Riley, and to all our children's future

Contents

Abbreviations

BBCC	Black Bear Conservation Committee
BCCP	Balcones Canyonlands Conservation Plan
BLM	Bureau of Land Management
CERCLA	Comprehensive Environmental Response, Compensation, and Liability Act
CITES	Convention on International Trade in Endangered Species of Wild Fauna and Flora
CRP	Conservation Reserve Program
CVM	Contingent valuation method
DOI	U.S. Department of the Interior
EPA	Environmental Protection Agency
ESA	Endangered Species Act
FWS	U.S. Fish and Wildlife Service
GAO	General Accounting Office
HCP	Habitat conservation plan
HTM	Habitat Transaction Method
IAFWA	International Association of Fish and Wildlife Agencies
IENR	Institute for Environment and Natural Resources (University of Wyoming)
IGBC	Interagency Grizzly Bear Committee
ITP	Incidental take permit
NAWCA	North American Wetlands Conservation Act
NAWMP	North American Waterfowl Management Plan
NCCP	Natural Community Conservation Planning

NEPA	National Environmental Policy Act
NMFS	National Marine Fisheries Service
NRC	National Research Council
NWF	National Wildlife Federation
OPL	Oklahoma Private Lands (initiative)
RCW	Red-cockaded woodpecker
TAMM	Timber Assessment Market Model
TDR	Tradable development rights
WGA	Western Governors' Association
WRP	Wetlands Reserve Program

Foreword

William D. Ruckelshaus

Rarely has a law with such humble beginnings had such a far-reaching effect on the American people as the Endangered Species Act. Likewise, it is remarkable that a law intended to rally public support around the preservation of deeply rooted American symbols such as the grizzly bear and the bald eagle can be so divisive in practice. Frequently, it pits well-intentioned landowners, many of whom care deeply about the land and its heritage, against equally well-intentioned conservationists and government officials.

There is widespread acknowledgment that the Endangered Species Act, passed by Congress in 1973, is in need of reform. For every species the Fish and Wildlife Service has removed from the endangered species list, it has added more than one hundred others. Those whose property is impacted by the law charge that it provides strong disincentives for hosting endangered species on private lands (where close to 90 percent of endangered species find habitat), and unfairly imposes the cost of preservation on a few for the benefit of the many. This is not to suggest that the law has not had notable successes; it has. The habitat conservation planning program, for example, has in some cases provided the necessary flexibility to accommodate the concerns of landowners while preserving the integrity of the act. But with Congress and the administration committed to reauthorization, there may be a rare opportunity to revisit and significantly improve upon the original law.

In the next several years, as a nation, we will either consciously or by default make many momentous decisions. Certainly the decision to prevent the permanent extinction of a species falls into this category. The Endangered Species Act is a strong national expression of a deep commitment to biodiversity. Yet we are not winning the fight against extinction. The increasing number of threatened species, despite almost twenty-five years of the ESA, is evidence that simply pledging support for the concept of conserving biodiversity is not enough. If we are serious about protecting species, we must commit adequate resources to underwrite the true cost of species protection, and spread these costs fairly and evenly among those realizing the benefits—the American public.

It is evident that the current system, despite certain strengths, is not presenting us with clear, honest choices of what we can preserve, what we must preserve, and how we can best accomplish it. As currently implemented, the ESA does not encourage enough discussion among parties with conflicting interests, and often results in delays, lawsuits, and too many disaffected citizens. This benefits no one, least of all the species in need of protection.

As we consider revisions to the Endangered Species Act, we should be careful not to confuse the assessment of risk, in this case the possibility of species loss, with the political decisions about how best to manage that possibility. Assessing the risk should be as pure a scientific exercise as possible. If the scientific decision to list a species as threatened or endangered automatically triggers regulatory actions, without leaving adequate room for discussion, flexibility, and tailoring solutions to local circumstances, this inevitably will result in attacks on the science. Clearly separating risk assessment and risk management will foster more publicly acceptable rendering of the science while laying the groundwork for a more open and honest discussion among affected parties regarding a fair and effective remedy.

There may be legitimate concerns that unless specific actions are automatically triggered by a scientific finding, nothing will be done to prevent a species from slipping into extinction. However, once a decision is made that a species is endangered, it is often counterproductive for government to attempt to control exactly what actions must be taken to preserve it. An increasing body of evidence in environmental regulation indicates that allowing flexibility in the means of attaining required performance goals is more likely to result in their successful achievement. Engaging citizens, industry, and governments at all levels in meaningful, collaborative discussion regarding how best to achieve the desired result can be far more effective than the rigid application of generic or prescribed rules/responses, and is more likely in the long term to result in the recovery and reestablishment of a species.

In fact, many collaborative decision-making processes for natural resource management have arisen spontaneously and in increasing numbers throughout the country. In some branches of the federal government, there is a growing willingness to allow the affected groups to settle their differences and make recommendations. This does not mean that public officials will abdicate their authority or responsibilities or that the overall goals of the ESA must be compromised. If designed properly, these cooperative efforts can supplement and amplify the democratic processes, and assist leaders in building the public support necessary to fashion and implement solutions.

For collaborative decision-making processes to work and their decisions to stick it is critical that all interests be included. One good example of a locally driven effort is found in the state of Washington. The state department of natural resources worked with local citizens on the Commission on Old Growth Alternatives to craft unprecedented consensus-based recommendations for managing state-owned old growth timber. Another example is in Montana, where the Clark Fork Basin Committee developed recommendations—later incorporated into statute by the Montana legislature—to resolve disputes over instream flow and water rights in the Clark Fork River.

These and many other examples illustrate that collaborative decision making offers a path out of gridlock. By no means is this a panacea for every environmental problem. A well-constructed process can require a great deal of time and patience from the participants. It does not always work. But it is vital that we develop settings where people can learn the habit of listening before passing judgment—not the typical public meeting where people state their positions and afterward are under no obligation to listen to any other statements. In cooperative processes, you *have* to listen to the other side. Even if consensus is not achieved, useful work is accomplished by identifying those areas where consensus is possible and uncovering those areas where more work, possibly more research or creative thinking, must be done.

We have learned that ordinary citizens have the ability to filter through scientific information that may contain contradictions and come up with reasonable findings. Economics have to be confronted in some detail.

These processes are ultimately about who gets what—the genius lies in discovering that different sides can each get what they need, and that the pie can be artfully cut so as to be bigger than we thought. We must find ways to move, for example, from saying jobs *or* wildlife to saying jobs *and* wildlife.

One of the keys to making all this work lies in restoring an ingredient that is lacking or nonexistent in many of these disputes: trust—trust in the ability of democratic institutions to adapt and meet the real needs of those who rely on them; trust in government officials who by law are the custodians and trustees of the public welfare; trust in unbiased and sound science to provide underpinnings and parameters and dispel myths that lead to irrational and costly decisions or even hysteria; and at least a modicum of trust that those with opposing or different viewpoints are not manipulating or distorting facts to achieve their own ends.

This restoration of trust, and the creation of a forum where such trust among traditional adversaries can germinate and take root, was a primary purpose for the establishment of the Institute for Environment and Natural Resources at the University of Wyoming.

The policy board of the institute, comprised of citizens and leaders from government, industry, academia, ranching, and the environmental community, devoted its May 1996 forum to one particular aspect of the Endangered Species Act: protection of species on private land. A thorough, well-researched set of background papers was prepared by faculty from the University of Wyoming and outside experts, with assistance and direction from policy board members. These papers fulfilled a critical need for accurate information and provided a sound underpinning for the scientific, technical, and policy issues considered by the board.

The board set about the task of developing a set of principles that would benefit those directly impacted by the ESA and would help guide policymakers during reauthorization discussions of private property issues. The resulting recommendations acknowledge that there are wide variations of opinion regarding the impact of the ESA on landowners and the effectiveness of the act. Despite these differences, a diverse group— after sometimes impassioned discussion—was able to agree that early and meaningful involvement of stakeholders, flexibility in achieving goals, and proactive management of habitat to prevent the need for species listings would markedly improve our current approach to protecting species.

The institute's goal is to assist in the development of farsighted, balanced, and comprehensive solutions to environmental and natural resource conflicts, based on good science and tempered by realistic policy considerations. The work presented in this book is part of the institute's continuing efforts to advance solutions to conflicts arising from implementation of the ESA on private property.

NOTE

William D. Ruckelshaus is Chairman, Browning-Ferris Industries, Inc., and Principal, Madrona Investment Group, L.L.C. A graduate of Princeton University and Harvard Law School, Mr. Ruckelshaus was the first administrator of the U.S. Environmental Protection Agency, 1970–1973, and served again in the same position in 1983–1984.

Preface

This book originated from research commissioned by the policy board of the Institute for Environment and Natural Resources at the University of Wyoming. To support its May 1996 forum, Private Property and the Endangered Species Act, the policy board asked the authors to examine what was known and unknown about endangered species on private land. Revised versions of these papers make up Chapters 2 through 6. The authors wrote for a general audience because the board reflects a broad spectrum of American society; its members come from government, industry, academia, and the environmental community, and they represent diverse state, regional, national, and international interests and expertise. After reading the papers and discussing species and property from varied niches, the board defined a set of principles to help frame the ongoing Endangered Species Act reauthorization debate. These principles are found in Chapter 7. Versions of the original papers and principles were published in *Land and Water Law Review* (volume 32, number 2, 1997). The authors have revised the papers for this book, and I have added a short introduction to accent common threads.

Thanks to Bill Gern and Kathie Cuomo at the IENR for their support, and to Steve Gloss and Tom Crocker for their direction and motivation. Ann Mullens Boelter deserves extra praise for her intelligent and persistent research support throughout the project. As always, I am indebted to family—Deb, Maija, and Riley—and friends for their relief and shelter.

JFS
Centennial, Wyoming
March 1998

Private Property and the Endangered Species Act

❧ 1 ❧

Introduction

Jason F. Shogren

Congress passed the Endangered Species Act of 1973 to shelter threatened and endangered species from the pressures of economic activity on private and public land. They recognized that species have "ecological, educational, historical, recreational and scientific value" unaccounted for in the course of "economic growth and development" (ESA, Section 2). But the act has proven controversial—the benefits of protecting endangered species accrue to the entire nation, while many of the costs accrue only to private landowners. As of this writing, some 1,125 species of plants and animals are listed as endangered or threatened under the ESA (see Table 1.1). In 1993, about 90 percent of the 781 species listed at that time had some or all of their habitat on nonfederal lands,[1] the majority of which were private lands. Many landowners complain that the costs of complying are too high. Broad benefits and concentrated costs fan most political fires, and public pressure to know whether these costs exceed the social benefits has turned up the heat in the ESA reauthorization debate.

The heat is generated from two antithetical beliefs. First, the advocates of species recovery argue that assessing the risk to endangered species is a question best left to the natural sciences—risk is first quantified, and then habitat is managed. This view relegates individual choices and the relevant economic and social parameters to the management stage, in which recovery efforts constrain individual land-use decisions. Second, the advocates of private property believe that since individual sovereignty

Table 1.1. *Box Score of Threatened and Endangered Species (as of 31 December 1997)*

Group	Endangered U.S.	Endangered Foreign	Threatened U.S.	Threatened Foreign	Total Species	Species with Plans
Mammals	57	251	7	16	331	39
Birds	75	178	15	6	274	72
Reptiles	14	65	20	14	113	30
Amphibians	9	8	7	1	25	11
Fishes	67	11	41	0	119	78
Snails	15	1	7	0	23	18
Clams	56	2	6	0	64	45
Crustaceans	16	0	3	0	19	7
Insects	28	4	9	0	41	21
Arachnids	5	0	0	0	5	4
Animal subtotal	**342**	**520**	**115**	**37**	**1,014**	**330**
Flowering plants	525	1	113	0	639	390
Conifers	2	0	0	2	4	1
Ferns & others	26	0	2	0	28	22
Plant subtotal	**553**	**1**	**115**	**2**	**671**	**413**
Grand total	**895**	**521**	**230**	**39**	**1,685**	**743** *

Total U.S. Endangered:	**895**
Total U.S. Threatened:	**230**
Total U.S. Species:	**1,125**

Source: United States Fish and Wildlife Service, Division of Endangered Species (1997).

* There are 477 approved recovery plans—some plans cover more than one species, and some species have more than one plan.

is the foundation of social order in the United States, a person should be left alone to make his or her own choices on allocating his or her private resources. The idea that we should further restrict this sovereignty with some form of institutional sovereignty such as the ESA that allows presumably better informed policymakers to make resource allocation decisions independent of individual valuations has upset many landowners.

But neither view captures the complexity of the debate. The risk assessment-management bifurcation is unjustified, both by intuition and policy that requires recovery priority rankings to consider the degree of conflict with development. And while Ruckelshaus makes the correct point that normative politics should be excluded, risk assessment does require positive input from both the physical and economic systems that provide the means of choice. Species are more likely to be endangered the greater the conflict with development activities; species are less threatened the greater the conservation efforts. Since development and conservation decisions depend on economic parameters such as relative prices and income, so does the risk of extinction. But of course complete control over private property has never been a reality either. Property rights come with obligations and responsibilities defined by law and refined through the courts. This point is unmistakably illustrated in Feldman and Brennan's detailed discussion of ESA case law in Chapter 3. Whether private markets can be shaped by case law to account for successful endangered species protection remains to be seen. A careful evaluation of the ground between the two beliefs is needed. Effective protection of endangered species requires evaluation of both natural science and economic parameters that affect the accurate estimation of risk and the effective management of needed habitat. As such, a major research priority is to gain more insight into the links between species protection and private property.

This book explores the connection between endangered species protection and private property in the United States. Our objective is to provide fair-minded content to the ongoing ESA debates, with the hope of supplying more light than heat on this already contentious issue. The common thread that underlies the discussion throughout the book is the interaction, divergence, and potential opportunities between private choice and public policy. The ESA links to private economic actions because it can be used to constrain the actions of private parties and public agencies; the subsequent decisions of private parties affect the risks to endangered species. Economic and biological systems affect each other, and policymakers must understand the links to design incentives that will match private actions to social desires, as discussed by Lockwood in Chapter 5.

In Chapter 2, Anderson notes that the administrative process supporting the ESA involves listing a species as threatened or endangered, designating critical habitats for its survival, prohibiting activities that accelerate extinction, creating and executing a recovery plan, and removing a species from the list when it no longer is in danger. Under the current Section 9 of the ESA, when a listed species is found on private property, the landowner must manage this habitat such that he or she does not "take" the fish or wildlife species, where *take* means "to harass, harm, pursue, hunt, shoot, wound, kill, trap, capture, or collect, or to attempt to engage in any such conduct." If the current or proposed use of the private property is inconsistent with this directive, the landowner must either rethink his or her actions toward more benign activities or apply for an "incidental take" permit (Section 10).

The incidental take permit under Section 10 of the 1982 ESA Amendments authorized take that is incidental to otherwise lawful economic activities. A landowner wanting the incidental take permit must develop a habitat conservation plan that spells out the likely impacts; the measures to monitor, minimize, and mitigate any impacts; funding sources to undertake these measures; protocol to deal with surprises; alternative actions considered that would cause no take, and why these actions are not being used; and additional measures that the Fish and Wildlife Service and the National Marine Fisheries Service may require as necessary.[2] Regardless, the landowner usually does not receive full, if any, compensation for the lost opportunities from having to manage his or her land in ways compatible with the ESA.

For instance, in the Balcones Canyonlands Conservation Plan in the Hill Country of Texas where a 30,000-acre preserve was established for the golden-cheeked warbler, landowners within the preserve were offered an average of $5,500 an acre for land selling at $10,000 to $20,000 an acre previously. The specific arrangement was that developers using land outside the preserve paid a $5,500-per-acre mitigation fee that would then be used to buy one acre inside the preserve. Plus the BCCP gave the government twenty years to pay and obliged it to do so only if it actually had the money at any time during the twenty years. But since enough funds currently do not exist to buy the 30,000 acres within the preserve, no compensation has been paid to the private property owners for complying with the ESA.

In general, the ESA imposes economic costs on private landowners when a designation constrains productive activity that was unanticipated by the market. In Chapter 4, Shogren and Hayward discuss what is known about the magnitude of these economic costs. And although landowners could avoid economic loss by destroying potential habitat both before and after the species are listed, most have not. But property owners are angry because federal and state officials have the additional authority to impose land-use policies that restrict what they can do on their private property. Landowners have pushed back with such vigor that policymakers and natural scientists now willingly admit that any attempt to rewrite the ESA must explicitly address the nature of economic incentives.

For instance, in 1995, Interior Secretary Bruce Babbitt announced ten principles to improve implementation of the ESA: (1) treat landowners fairly and with consideration; (2) minimize social and economic impacts; (3) provide quick, responsive answers and certainty to landowners; (4) base ESA decisions on sound and objective scientific information; (5) prevent species from becoming endangered or threatened; (6) promptly recover and delist threatened or endangered species; (7) provide state, tribal, and local governments with opportunities to play a greater role in carrying out the ESA; (8) make effective use of limited public and private resources by focusing on groups of species dependent on the same habitat; (9) promote efficiency and consistency in the Departments of the Interior and Commerce; and (10) create incentives for landowners to conserve species. Eisner et al.[3] also include economic incentives in their wish lists of ways to fix the ESA.

Closing the gap between private choices and social goals will require more than wishful thinking about changing individual preferences—it will require a change in the relative costs of different actions. Various proposals to change costs by adding flexibility to the ESA have attempted to fill the void; as detailed by Turner and Rylander in Chapter 6, these include "safe harbors," tax relief, and tradable habitat permits. These flexibility measures are aimed at closing the gap between private and social perceptions of time and space. The endangered species agencies have launched a "no surprises" policy to reduce uncertainty to landowners who have filed a habitat conservation plan to qualify for incidental takings. If the habitat needs of a species change, these landowners are under no further obligation to meet the new needs. These agencies have also developed a safe harbor agreement—if a landowner agrees to manage his or her lands for a listed species, he or she is safe from any future restrictions if the population of the species increases and expands.

Economic incentives are also being considered as direct tools to close the private-social gap in perceptions. Numerous proposals have been made that would add a compensatory or insurance policy to the ESA— people would receive compensation for or would be insured against losses suffered under the ESA. This would reduce opposition to the ESA, deter the government from taking too much land, and encourage landowners to develop land in more socially efficient ways. But the risk of extensive litigation and concocted claims are potential downsides to some of the ill-conceived compensation schemes proposed in recent ESA reauthorization bills.[4] The agencies can also take a proactive role by identifying critical habitat for listed and unlisted species, and designing a voluntary compensation scheme for critical habitat that cuts across the holdings of several private landowners. Such a system should be voluntary, allow for a minimum probability of species survival, be flexible enough to accommodate a single large or several small reserves through the use of an acre-agglomeration bonus, provide incentives for the landowner to reveal his or her private information on his or her ability to make a profit from the land, and account for the deadweight loss of the funds used to compensate the landowner for setting aside his or her acres.[5]

In the end, the better we understand how economic and biological systems are linked, the fewer unpleasant choices we may have to make. Although the idea of extinction is inherently unacceptable to most people, a balanced understanding will be required because it is not obvious to everyone that encyclopedic species protection holds a moral trump card over economic growth to raise the standard of living for people alive today. Wise choices will require guidance from common principles such as those defined in Chapter 7 by the diverse policy board of the Institute of Environment and Natural Resources at the University of Wyoming.[6] Whether people choose to believe such principles will dictate whether the future of endangered species and private property will be dominated by conflict or cooperation.

NOTES

1   General Accounting Office, *Endangered Species Act: Information on Species Protection on Nonfederal Lands,* GAO/RCED-95-16 (Washington, D.C.: U.S. General Accounting Office, 1994).
2   Fish and Wildlife Service and National Marine Fisheries Service, *Making the ESA Work Better: Implementing the 10-Point Plan and Beyond* (Washington, D.C., 1997).

3   T. Eisner, J. Lubchenco, E. O. Wilson, D. Wilcove, and M. Bean, Building a Sci-
     entifically Sound Policy for Protecting Endangered Species, *Science* 268(1995):
     1231–1232.

     National Research Council, *Science and the Endangered Species Act* (Washing-
     ton, D.C.: National Academy of Sciences, 1996).

4   J. Goldstein, Whose Land Is It Anyway? *Choices,* 1996, second quarter, 4–8.

     C. Mann and M. Plummer, *Noah's Choice* (New York: A. Knopf, 1995).

5   R. Smith and J. Shogren, Voluntary Incentive Design for Endangered Species
     Protection, photocopy (Saint Paul: University of Minnesota, 1997).

     G. Brown and J. Shogren, Economics of the Endangered Species Act, *Journal
     of Economic Perspectives* (forthcoming).

6   The University of Wyoming established the Institute for Environment and Natu-
     ral Resources in 1993 to develop balanced research and policy solutions to envi-
     ronmental and natural resource issues. The institute is led by a policy board of
     leaders from government, industry, academia, and the environmental commu-
     nity, representing diverse state, regional, national, and international interests
     and expertise. A multidisciplinary research faculty from the University comple-
     ments the many different viewpoints on the board.

❊ 2 ❊

The Evolution of the Endangered Species Act

Stanley H. Anderson

Early visitors to the New World found an abundance of wildlife. For example, John Cabot noted the large number of fish in the eastern coastal area in 1500.[1] His son, Sebastian Cabot, later commented that fish were so abundant along the coastal waters that they could slow the progress of a ship.[2] Explorers on both coasts of the New World were amazed at the number and varieties of wildlife species. There was no problem finding sufficient food on land as people colonized the area and moved westward onto the continent. At the same time, commercial use of the wildlife resources began. Pelts and plumes brought high prices on the European markets, and trappers explored many parts of North America to find these valuable items.

Early conservation efforts began, oddly enough, as hunters and fishermen noted a decline in wildlife. In the mid-1800s, sport groups encouraged the federal government to maintain the wildlife resources in the United States. In 1872, President Grant set aside 8,671 square kilometers of land designated as a refuge for wildlife—the area would eventually become Yellowstone National Park. In 1885, the federal government set up a federal wildlife agency by funding the predecessor of the Biological Survey, now known as the Fish and Wildlife Service.[3]

EVOLUTION OF WILDLIFE LAW
AND THE ENDANGERED SPECIES ACT

Like any other form of resource management, wildlife management is based on legal documents and procedures. Wildlife law can be traced to various decisions and proclamations from the Roman Empire through feudal European history to the beginning of the United States as a sovereign nation. In England before the signing of the Magna Carta in 1215, wildlife was the property of the king, who granted hunting and fishing rights to the nobility. Later, Parliament assumed the right to control the harvest of wildlife. In the United States, federal statutes and regulations, executive orders, and treaties and other international agreements govern the action of federal agencies, while state laws, administrative orders, and court decisions provide the authorization for action at the state level.

In examining the legal basis for managing wildlife, one gets bewildered by the many interrelated, overlapping, and frequently ambiguous regulations. The situation has not been helped by the fact that the word *wildlife* has been difficult for the legal profession to define. European hunters originally associated the word only with the animals taken for food and sport. Today, however, *wildlife* includes nongame vertebrates and invertebrates as well.

Furthermore, wildlife does not observe human-drawn boundaries, although when an aquatic species comes near the shore of a country, that country may try to make regulations governing it. Within our country, many wildlife regulatory measures have been the subject of states' rights debates. Jurisdictional disputes between federal and state agencies have sometimes increased the difficulty of managing our wildlife resources.

Regulations in the United States

The Constitution is the ultimate source of authority for governmental actions in the United States. State and federal governments both look to the Constitution in establishing wildlife law. States generally have been given authority over wildlife that resides within their boundaries. States enforce hunting regulations, but they must abide by treaties on migratory species made by the federal government. The federal government can exercise control over fish and wildlife by virtue of the powers conferred on it in the Constitution and expressed in laws passed by Congress and interpretations of the courts.

The authority for conservation and protection of wildlife derives primarily from three legal sources. The first is statutory laws—laws enacted by Congress either for specific wildlife protection or for protection of resources, including wildlife. Specific wildlife legislative acts include the Bald Eagle Protection Act and Wild Free-Roaming Horses and Burro Act. Resource laws include the Clean Air Act, Water Pollution Control Act, National Wild and Scenic River Act, Solid Waste Disposal Act, Environmental Noise Control Act, Resource Conservation and Recovery Act, and National Environmental Policy Act.

Common law, which is the body of court decisions deriving from custom and traditional practices, is the second authority for wildlife regulations. Common laws affect wildlife in the areas of negligence, nuisance, and trespass. The right of a landowner to prevent access for hunting or fishing on private property falls under common law.

Case law is the third legal source. Legislative acts and common law are often written in general language, allowing a number of interpretations. Conflicts in the interpretation of common law are resolved in the courts, and the decisions of the courts become case law. Case law, which often reflects changes in people's attitudes, has constituted much of the authority for the federal government to control commerce in wildlife and to manage wildlife on federal lands. Courts resolve federal-state wildlife conflicts. The importance of case law is examined in detail in Chapter 3.

Treaties, Acts, and Related Laws

Table 2.1 summarizes treaties and acts upon which many wildlife and endangered species actions have been based. Other laws and decisions also influence wildlife management: zoning laws and permits that control or direct land development; leasing rights on federal and state lands, as well as access rights; and the regulatory mechanisms for land development and reclamation practices. When one works with wildlife, no one document furnishes all the answers; many regulations and documents must be considered. Thus, a good understanding of the many legal ramifications makes a wildlife manager more effective.

Table 2.1. *History of Wildlife and Endangered Species Regulation in the United States*

1900
Passage of the Lacey Act, which prohibited the interstate transportation of "any wild animals or birds" killed in violation of state law. The act upheld the authority of a state to prohibit the export of game lawfully killed in the state and allowed the states to prohibit the importation of game. It also authorized the secretary of agriculture to adopt measures necessary for the "preservation, distribution, introduction, and restoration of game birds and other wild birds," subject to laws of the various states and territories.

1916
The Convention for the Protection of Migratory Birds was signed between the United States and Great Britain (signing for Canada). A group of migratory birds listed with the convention was specifically protected. The convention allowed for the establishment of open hunting seasons on game birds and provided protection for nongame birds. It prohibited taking nests or eggs except for scientific or propagation purposes.

1926
The Black Bass Act was passed and later amended to regulate importation and transportation of black bass and other fish.

1934
Passage of the Fish and Wildlife Coordination Act, which specifically emphasized the impact of water development projects on wildlife.

1936
Treaty for the conservation of migratory birds, similar to the 1916 treaty with Great Britain, signed with Mexico.

1940
A convention on the nature, protection, and preservation of wildlife in the Western Hemisphere was signed by the United States and eleven other American republics. This treaty expressed the wish of governments to "protect and conserve their natural habitats for wildlife and to preserve representatives of all species in general of their native flora and fauna including migratory birds" and to protect regions and natural areas of scientific value. The nations agreed to take certain actions to achieve these objectives, including "appropriate measures for the protection of migratory birds of economic or aesthetic value or to prevent the threatened extinction of any given species."

1964
The FWS organized a Rare and Endangered Species Committee, which prepared
the first U.S. "redbook" on *Rare and Endangered Fish and Wildlife of the United States*
(Washington, D.C.: Bureau of Sport Fisheries and Wildlife, 1966). Although no
formal legal status or protection was afforded to species included in this book, the
Committee's efforts served to inform people of the plight of selected animals and
give federal recognition to the problem.

1966
Passage of the Endangered Species Preservation Act, which directed the FWS to
prepare and maintain an official list of endangered native animals. Although this
act provided no authority to regulate taking or trade, it did authorize funds for
management and research for listed species. Land and water conservation funds
were made available to acquire endangered species habitat.

1967
Establishment of the Office of Endangered Species to administer the Endangered
Species Preservation Act. The first official list of endangered native animals, con-
sisting of seventy-eight vertebrates, was published.

1969
The 1966 act was amended by passage of the Endangered Species Conservation
Act, which gave the FWS new authority to list mollusks and foreign species and
to regulate their import. Protection was also soon provided for listed native species. The secretaries of agriculture, defense, and the interior were directed to use
their authority consistent with other mandates to conserve and protect endangered species. The FWS initiated a process of recovery plans in the early 1970s.
The implementing document was designed to outline a step-by-step program for
recovery of a species.

1969
Passage of the National Environmental Policy Act (NEPA), establishing the policy
that federal decision making should include evaluating the effects of federal
actions on the quality of the human environment.

1972
Treaty for the conservation of migratory birds, similar to the 1916 treaty with
Great Britain, signed with Japan.

1973
Ratification of the Convention on International Trade in Endangered Species of
Wild Fauna and Flora (CITES).

1973
Passage of the Endangered Species Act, which brought U.S. policy into line with CITES, and greatly increased the authority and scope of the U.S. program. Responsibility for implementing the ESA was divided between the secretary of commerce (for most marine species) and the secretary of the interior (for all other species). The secretary of agriculture was given responsibility for enforcement of import/export controls for listed plants.

The ESA recognized "threatened" species, to provide protection for species before they were in imminent danger of extinction. The ESA also provided listing of any vertebrate or invertebrate, not just members of selected classes, as in the 1969 act. Listing of plant species was allowed, as was listing of animal populations, not just specific species or subspecies.

Public participation was encouraged in the listing or delisting process. The ESA allowed people to request a public hearing in addition to the normal public comment period. It also allowed any person to bring action in the U.S. District Court for alleged violation of the ESA. The court may prohibit any person or agency (including the FWS) from conducting acts deemed harmful to endangered species.

The purposes of the ESA are to conserve ecosystems upon which endangered and threatened species depend, to provide a program for the conservation of such endangered and threatened species, and to take appropriate steps to achieve the purposes of the treaties and conventions set forth in the ESA.

1977
FWS clarifies treaties on migratory birds by publishing a list of species covered.

1978
A convention with the Union of Soviet Socialist Republics on the Conservation of Migratory Birds and Their Environment was concluded.

Acquisition of Wildlife Habitat

Use of more than one-third of the nation's land is controlled by agencies of the federal government. Under the property clause of the Constitution, the federal government has broad powers over these lands, including the management of wildlife. While the National Wildlife Refuge System is the only extensive federally owned land system managed exclusively for wildlife, many legislative acts empower the federal government to manage wildlife on other federal lands. The U.S. Forest Service, U.S. Bureau of Land Management, and other land-management agencies must consider preservation of fish and wildlife in researching land-use decisions. States have legislation related to management of wildlife on state-owned property.

The Migratory Bird Treaty Act (1918) was a stimulus to establish a systematic program of refuge acquisition. The original act did not provide for the acquisition of habitat, a deficiency remedied by a 1929 amendment. The Migratory Bird Hunting Stamp Act (1934) provided funding for land acquisition, and the result was the establishment of a series of wildlife refuges along major migratory bird routes. Originally designed primarily to protect migratory waterfowl, the refuges came to serve many species of animals.

Several other laws allowed acquisition of land for wildlife, for example, the Fish and Wildlife Coordination Act (1934), the Land and Water Conservation Fund Act (1965), and the Endangered Species Act. The Land and Water Conservation Fund Act has been the major act providing for land acquisition.[4]

Acquisition of land by the federal government has become difficult because of political pressure. Private conservation agencies, such as the Nature Conservancy and Ducks Unlimited, have bought or received donations of land that can be used for wildlife. The Nature Conservancy has owned more than 250,000 ha (617,750 acres) in the 1990s and often acts as a middleman, buying and holding land until a public agency can complete the purchase or assume management. Acquisition by a conservation agency or organization remains the best and perhaps the most favored method of maintaining wildlife habitat, especially wetlands. Nonprofit private conservation organizations are taking an increasingly important part in advising which wildlife habitats to purchase. Converting private holdings to public ownership has been effective in the Midwest and East, where few public lands were reserved.

It is not always necessary or desirable to take full ownership of land and water to preserve wildlife; acquisition of easements or development rights may often get the desired results. Easements involve greatly reduced initial outlay and lower management expense. The FWS has approximately 942,000 ha (2,327,685 acres) under lease or easement, and more than half the acreage in waterfowl protection areas has been acquired through easements.

Land-use zoning, the control of privately owned real estate by public law, came into practice in 1916. Zoning is an exercise of police power, and though it was first used to prevent such nuisances as the slaughtering of horses in residential neighborhoods, it has been expanded to control land for many public benefits. Zoning has been effectively used to maintain wildlife habitats in a number of states. Alaska, for instance, has developed a coastal management program with land-use control, and the California coastal management program allows the zoning of special areas, providing significant wildlife habitats such as forests, wetlands, estuaries, and streams.[5]

GOAL OF THE ENDANGERED SPECIES ACT

Recovery is the cornerstone and ultimate purpose of the Endangered Species Act. Recovery is the process by which the decline of an endangered or threatened species is arrested or reversed, and threats to its survival are neutralized, so that its long-term survival in nature can be ensured. The goal of this process is to restore listed species to a point where they are secure, self-sustaining components of their ecosystem so as to allow delisting.

As a result, ecosystems upon which endangered and threatened species depend may be conserved. The ESA provides a program for conservation and management of such species and their habitat. In this light, purposes of treaties and other legislation governing wildlife are also met.

PROVISIONS OF THE ENDANGERED SPECIES ACT

Originally passed in 1973, the ESA has been reauthorized and amended a number of times. The act says that its intent is to conserve various species of plants and animals in conjunction with:

1 migratory bird treaties with Canada and Mexico;
2 the Migratory and Endangered Bird Treaty with Japan;
3 the Convention on Nature Protection and Wildlife Preservation in the Western Hemisphere;
4 the International Convention for the Northwest Atlantic Fisheries;
5 the International Convention for the High Seas Fisheries of the North Pacific Ocean;
6 the Convention on International Trade in Endangered Species of Wild Fauna and Flora; and
7 other international agreements.

The ESA encourages states and other interested parties, through federal financial assistance and a system of incentives, to develop and maintain conservation programs that meet national and international standards. This is instrumental in meeting the international commitments of the United States and in better safeguarding the nation's heritage of fish, wildlife, and plants for the benefit of all citizens.

Section 2 deals with the purpose of the act, Section 3 with definitions, and Section 4 describes the listing process, the designation of "critical habitat," and recovery plans.

Section 5 allows the secretaries of the interior and agriculture to acquire, by purchase or donation, land, water, or interests therein to conserve fish, wildlife, and plants.

Section 6 indicates that maximum cooperation with the states shall occur. This cooperation shall include consultation and evaluation of concerns before acquisitions of lands and establishment of management and cooperative agreements.

For state management programs and cooperative agreements to remain active for the conservation of endangered and threatened species, the secretary of the interior must find and reconfirm each year that the following criteria are met:

1   the species that is threatened or endangered is found in the state, and the state conservation agency has authority to manage the species;
2   "the state conservation agency has established acceptable conservation programs, consistent with the purposes and policies of this Act, for all resident species of fish or wildlife in the state which are deemed by the Secretary to be endangered or threatened, and has furnished a copy of such plan and program together with all pertinent details, information, and data requested to the Secretary" (Section 6[c][1][B]);
3   "the state agency is authorized to conduct investigations to determine the status and requirements for survival of resident species of fish and wildlife" (Section 6[c][1][C]); and
4   "the state agency is authorized to establish programs, including the acquisition of land or aquatic habitat or interests therein, for the conservation of resident endangered or threatened species of fish or wildlife" (Section 6[c][1][D]).

Section 7 describes federal actions and interagency cooperation. All actions that might impact on listed or proposed species must be reviewed by the secretary of the interior. This includes species that occur on federal land under the jurisdiction of the Department of the Interior or species on private land that might be impacted by federal agency action.

If an action by a federal agency is likely to impact an endangered, threatened, or proposed species, a biological assessment must be made. This assessment should determine the presence or absence of the endangered species, as well as its status and the extent, if any, to which the action may affect the continued existence in the wild of that species.

As a result of the assessment, the secretary may concur with the active agency that there is minimal or even a positive impact and conclude that the action can go ahead. But if an endangered, threatened, or proposed species may be impacted, the active agency must initiate consultation with the secretary. If the agencies reach a solution, the action may proceed with reasonable and prudent alternatives. If the agencies cannot reach an agreement, a jeopardy statement is issued with no alternatives; however, this has rarely occurred. That means that several suggestions must be put forth on alternative ways to proceed with the proposed action. For example, placing telescopes on Mount Graham in southern Arizona could have impacted the endangered Mount Graham red squirrel.[6] An alterna-tive was to place the telescopes on a nearby mountain.

If an impasse occurs and agreement cannot be reached on an action that could jeopardize the continued existence of the species in the wild, an individual organization may apply for an exemption. The act calls for the establishment of an Endangered Species Committee to review the funding and recommend action. The committee shall be composed of seven members:

1 the secretary of agriculture;
2 the secretary of the army;
3 the chairman of the Council of Economic Advisers;
4 the administrator of the Environmental Protection Agency;
5 the secretary of the interior;
6 the administrator of the National Oceanic and Atmospheric Adminis-tration; and
7 the president, after consideration of any recommendations, shall appoint one individual from each affected state, as determined by the secretary of the interior, to be a member of the committee.

The committee would consider the application to exempt an agency ac-tion not later than thirty days after an application is submitted. There have been few requests for this so-called god squad in the history of the ESA.

Section 8, the international component of the ESA, implements the provisions of the Convention on International Trade in Endangered Species of Wild Fauna and Flora, or CITES. Besides encouraging endangered species conservation worldwide, this section also directs the president to implement the Convention on Natural Protection and Wildlife Preservation in the Western Hemisphere. In addition, ESA directs the secretary of the interior to encourage foreign nations to establish and carry out endangered species programs of their own and authorizes both financial assistance and the loan of federal wildlife personnel. Finally, the ESA authorizes the secretary of the interior to conduct law enforcement investigations and prohibits the importation of endangered and threatened species.

Section 9 lists various prohibited acts:

1   import or export of listed species;
2   removal of any listed species, or any harm, harassment, or disturbance of the listed species;
3   deliver, receive, carry or transport an endangered species; and
4   possess, sell, or transport in interstate commerce any endangered species.

Section 10 describes how exemptions to the Section 9 prohibitions may be obtained through permits from the FWS or National Marine Fisheries Service. These permits allow for the "incidental take" of listed species during otherwise lawful activities or in conjunction with an approved habitat conservation plan.

Other components to the ESA discuss actions that are prohibited, exceptions, law enforcement, endangered plants, and appropriations. These components are combined to become the endangered species program of the FWS and the NMFS.[7]

The ESA gives relatively broad power to the federal government to manage wildlife and wildlife habitats where endangered species are involved. The ESA directs the government to become involved with other nations in preventing the extinction of endangered species.

The provisions of the ESA are enforced in different ways. If an endangered species is found on public property or if a federal agency is involved in an activity on private property that might affect an endangered species, Section 7 applies. The federal agency must consult with the FWS and try to reach an agreement to avoid adversely impacting the species.

If a private person tries to harm, harass, remove, or destroy a listed species on public or private property, Section 9 applies. That person is subject to fines and/or jail sentences. Federal and state wildlife law enforcement personnel usually investigate such incidents.

On private property, Section 9 also applies. If a property owner goes about his or her activities so listed animals are not harmed, harassed, removed, or destroyed, there is no impact on the property owner. If a property owner does harm, harass, remove, or destroy an endangered species, federal and state law enforcement agents may bring charges against the property owner.

HOW DO SPECIES GET LISTED?

Species

The FWS or NMFS may nominate a species for listing as endangered or threatened, and an individual or organization may petition to initiate the listing process. A petition may be filed with the Department of the Interior or Commerce by anyone who has adequate data to support a proposed listing. The process begins with a letter to the secretary. For a species to be listed as an endangered or threatened species, evidence must be provided that its existence is in peril from one or more of the following:

1 the destruction or threatened destruction, modification, or curtailment of its habitat or range;
2 its overutilization for commercial, sport, scientific, or educational purposes;
3 disease or predation;
4 absence of regulatory mechanisms adequate to prevent its decline or the degradation of its habitat; and
5 other natural or human-made factors affecting its continued existence.

After the petition is received there is a ninety-day period during which the secretary shall make a finding as to whether the petition presents substantial scientific or commercial information indicating that the petitioned action may be warranted. If adequate information exists to consider the species for listing, the secretary must undertake a process in the next twelve months to determine if that listing is warranted, not warranted, or precluded by pending proposals. To make its recommendation, the FWS or NMFS follows what is known as a rule-making (or regulatory) procedure. This process is followed by all federal agencies in proposing regulations that will have the effect of law.

When the biological evidence concerning a species' status is not enough to justify a listing, the process may begin with the publication of a notice of review and solicitation of more information on the species from any source. This information, together with already gathered data, is published in the *Federal Register*. When the information is sufficient to warrant listing consideration, the Department of the Interior or Department of Commerce publishes in the *Federal Register* a proposal to list the animal or plant as endangered or threatened and to designate an appropriate critical habitat for the species. If the FWS or NMFS feels that listing is not warranted, the process stops.

At this and every other stage in the listing process, all interested persons are asked to comment on the proposal. Generally, a period of sixty days is allowed for public comment to discuss the proposal. To make sure that all interested members are aware of the proposal, news releases and special mailings are sent to inform the public, scientific community, other federal agencies, as well as state and county governments.

Delisting or reclassifying occurs when it is determined that a species has recovered sufficiently and follows in reverse the same procedure as the listing process. Each of the criteria for listing must be addressed, with evidence that the threats to the species that caused its listing have been addressed and eliminated.

Habitat

Designations of "critical habitat" under Section 4 of the ESA affect activities and are made primarily to help federal agencies locate endangered species and fulfill their responsibilities under the act. Critical habitat can be more than previously occupied habitat. It includes those areas of land, water, and air space that are required for the normal needs and survival of the occupying species at the time of its listing:

1   space for individual and population growth with normal behavior;
2   food, water, air, light, minerals, and other nutritional or physiological needs;
3   adequate cover or shelter;

4   sites for breeding, reproduction, rearing offspring, germination, or seed dispersal; and
5   protection from disturbances in a location representative of the historic, geographic, and ecological distribution of the listed species.

Certain areas may be excluded from the critical habitat designation if the secretary of the interior or secretary of commerce decides that the economic benefits outweigh the benefits of conserving the areas. Such areas are not to be excluded, however, if doing so would result in extinction of the species in the wild. Following the public comment period and public meetings on a proposal to list a species and its critical habitat, the information received is examined and, based on the best available biological data, a final decision is published. The ruling generally becomes effective thirty days after publication in the *Federal Register*.

Recovery Plans

To restore a protected species to its nonendangered status, the FWS is required to develop a recovery plan for each species listed. Recovery plans are prepared by a knowledgeable person on a voluntary or contract basis through a public or private agency or by a recovery team appointed by the FWS for that purpose. The elaborateness of recovery plans naturally depends on the range and characteristics of the species as well as the state of scientific knowledge about the species. For migratory species such as the whooping crane, or secretive mammals like the black-footed ferret, the plans can be quite complex.

Each recovery plan starts with background information on the species, its habitat, and its biological needs. The plan will cover possible manipulation of habitat, cleanup of habitat, transplantation, captive breeding programs, habitat acquisition, and recommendations to state, federal, and private agencies for changes in land-use practices. An implementation guide is developed, and the overall plan is approved by the Department of the Interior or Commerce and initiated.

Section 4 of the ESA directs that in developing and implementing recovery plans, the secretary should, to the maximum extent feasible, give priority to listed species that are most likely to benefit from such plans. Particular attention is given to species whose conservation may conflict with economic activity. Thus the FWS assigns recovery priority rankings, ranging from 1 to 18, to listed species according to the degree of threats, recovery potential, and taxonomic distinctness.[8] A species' rank may be elevated by adding the designation "C" to the numerical rank to indicate there is some conflict between recovery efforts and economic development. High priority rankings of 1, 1C, 2, or 2C are given to species of most concern with the highest potential for recovery. (See Chapter 4 for discussion of the effectiveness of recovery plans.)

Candidate Species

The 1988 amendments to the Endangered Species Act allowed the FWS to spend money toward the recovery of plant and animal species it has identified as candidates for listing as endangered or threatened. These amendments put wildlife and plants into a priority ranking based on categories. Category 1 species are those for which the FWS has enough information to support listing as soon as time and resources allow the developing and publishing of the requisite regulations in the *Federal Register*. Category 2 species are those for which there is some evidence of vulnerability, but for which there are not enough data to support listing proposals until status reviews can be done better.

Category 3, which has since been replaced by the "candidate species" list, was a compilation of those species that have been suggested at one time or another as possibly being in need of protection. It was subdivided into three parts: Category 3A, species thought to be extinct; Category 3B, those found to be taxonomically invalid; and Category 3C, those found no longer to be subject to substantial threats.

On 28 February 1996, the FWS issued a revised list of candidate species. The revised notice identifies 182 species as "candidates" for listing. "Candidate species" are species for which the FWS has enough information to warrant proposing them for listing as endangered or threatened. The revised candidate list replaces the old system that listed nearly 3,700 candidates.[9] Under the revised list, only those species for which there is enough information to support listing will be called "candidates." They were formerly known as Category 1 candidate species, with the highest priority ranking. The FWS will no longer maintain a Category 2 list. This will avoid the mistaken conclusion that the addition of thousands of species to the endangered list is imminent.

In September 1997, the FWS published a new revised Candidate Notice of Review naming 207 species that may warrant protection under the ESA.[10] This notice was published primarily to solicit new information on the status of candidate species and threats. Inclusion on the list of candidates does not guarantee that a species will automatically be listed as threatened or endangered.

CONCLUSIONS

This chapter has presented a brief overview of the evolution of wildlife law in the United States and how we got to the current status of the Endangered Species Act. For more detailed discussions, see Anderson,[11] Bean,[12] and the NRC.[13]

Perhaps the greatest concern raised by the ESA is that all species, subspecies, and populations are part of the ecosystem in which they live. When species decline, something is wrong with the system. Solutions lie in applying the best knowledge to maintain the species in a viable ecosystem. People must work effectively together and the public must be provided with reliable information to maximize our recovery efforts.

NOTES

1   T. L. Kimball and R. E. Johnson, The Richness of American Wildlife, in *Wildlife in America,* ed. H. P. Brokaw (Washington, D.C.: Council on Environmental Quality, 1978).

2   S. E. Morison, *The European Discovery of America: The Northern Voyages, A.D. 500–1600* (New York: Oxford University Press, 1971).

3   S. H. Anderson, *Managing Our Wildlife Resources,* 2d ed. (Englewood Cliffs, N.J.: Prentice Hall, 1991).

4   M. J. Bean, *The Evolution of National Wildlife Law* (New York: Praeger, 1983).

5   Anderson, *Managing Our Wildlife Resources.*

6   M. M. Waldrop, The Long, Sad Saga of Mount Graham, *Science* 248(1990): 1479–1481.

7   Fish and Wildlife Service, *Endangered Species Act of 1973 as Amended through the 100th Congress* (Washington, D.C.: Department of the Interior, 1992).

8   FWS, *Report to Congress: Recovery Program for Endangered and Threatened Species* (Washington, D.C.: Fish and Wildlife Service, 1994).

9   C. R. Groves, Candidate and Sensitive Species Programs, in *Endangered Species Recovery: Finding the Lessons, Improving the Process,* ed. T. W. Clark, R. P. Reading, and A. L. Clarke, pp. 227–250 (Washington, D.C.: Island Press, 1994).

10 Department of the Interior, Fish and Wildlife Service, Endangered and Threatened Wildlife and Plants: Review of Plant and Animal Taxa That Are Candidates

or Proposed for Listing as Endangered or Threatened, *Federal Register* 62/
182(1997):49398–49411.

11   Anderson, *Managing Our Wildlife Resources*.
12   Bean, *The Evolution of National Wildlife Law*.
13   National Research Council, *Science and the Endangered Species Act* (Washington,
D.C.: National Academy Press, 1995).

✾ 3 ✾

Judicial Application of the Endangered Species Act and the Implications for Takings of Protected Species and Private Property

Murray D. Feldman and Michael J. Brennan

INTRODUCTION

The substantive provisions of the Endangered Species Act have been construed by the United States Supreme Court on only two occasions.[1] The range of these Supreme Court decisions, separated by seventeen years, mirrors the evolution in the application of the ESA. In *TVA v. Hill*,[2] the Court enjoined the construction of the Tellico Dam to protect the snail darter, based in part on what the Court perceived to be congressional intent to reverse the trend of species extinction, "whatever the cost." The Court observed that

[i]t may seem curious to some that the survival of a relatively small number of three-inch fish among all the countless millions of species extant would require the permanent halting of a virtually completed dam for which Congress has expended more than $100 million. . . . We conclude, however, that the explicit provisions of the Endangered Species Act require precisely that result.

This decision demonstrates the initial focus of both ESA litigation and the agency application of the statute. In the early years of the program, the agencies implementing the act, the public, and reviewing courts largely focused on individual species and specific projects.

In *Babbitt v. Sweet Home Chapter of Communities for a Great Oregon,*[3] the Supreme Court upheld the FWS's regulatory interpretation of the Section 9 prohibition on taking listed species to apply to significant habitat modification activities on nonfederal land. In doing so, the Court noted that

> the broad purpose of the ESA supports the Secretary's decision to extend protection against activities that cause the precise harms Congress enacted the statute to avoid. . . . [A]mong its central purposes is "to provide a means whereby the ecosystems upon which endangered species and threatened species depend may be conserved." . . . [A]s all recognize, the Act encompasses a vast range of economic and social enterprises and endeavors.

The Court's *Sweet Home* decision reflects the shift in administration of the ESA—with the growing focus on concepts of conservation biology, biodiversity, and ecosystem management—to the conservation and management of multiple species and habitats as a common denominator.

This shifting focus for judicial application of the ESA has laid the foundation for discussions concerning changes to the act's implementation for two interrelated yet distinct aspects: the scope of takings of listed species prohibited by Section 9, and the constitutional limits of ESA regulation of private property without just compensation. This chapter examines the background of these two components of the debate over application and reauthorization of the ESA. First, we outline the ESA statutory framework to better understand where the species-taking provisions come into play, and also to identify potential sources of government regulatory authority that could lead to an uncompensated taking of private property. Second, we survey the development of the act's application through the case law to illustrate the growing focus on habitat and ecosystem conservation. Third, we highlight some of the current issues in ascertaining whether habitat-altering activities may constitute a prohibited Section 9 taking of protected species. Lastly, we describe the Fifth Amendment constitutional takings framework and evaluate its potential application to ESA regulatory actions.

THE STATUTORY FRAMEWORK

Application of the Endangered Species Act is triggered by the listing of a species under Section 4.[4] The ESA protects "endangered" species (those in danger of extinction throughout all or a significant portion of their range) and "threatened" species (those likely to become endangered within the foreseeable future). The federal agencies responsible for implementing the ESA are the Fish and Wildlife Service of the Department of the Interior, and the National Marine Fisheries Service of the Department of Commerce.[5] If a species is listed under Section 4, the agency generally must also designate "critical habitat" for the species. Critical habitat includes those areas essential to the conservation of a listed species that require special management or protection.

ESA Section 7 requires federal agencies to consult with the appropriate service to determine whether agency action may affect listed species or their habitat. An "action" is defined broadly to include "all activities or programs of any kind authorized, funded, or carried out, in whole or in part, by federal agencies in the United States or upon the high seas," including the "granting of licenses, contracts, leases, easements, rights-of-way, permits, or grants-in-aid."[6] Section 7 proscribes federal agencies from taking any action that is likely to jeopardize the continued existence of any listed species or result in the destruction or adverse modification of designated critical habitat. If the agency determines that its action will affect listed species or critical habitat, it must undertake formal consultation with the service.[7]

The product of the consultation process is generally a biological opinion issued by the FWS or NMFS indicating whether or not the action is likely to jeopardize the continued existence of a listed species or result in the destruction or adverse modification of critical habitat (a "jeopardy" opinion), or is not likely to result in such effects (a "no jeopardy" opinion).[8] A jeopardy biological opinion must include reasonable and prudent alternatives, if any, that would alter the action to avoid the likelihood of jeopardizing a listed species or resulting in the destruction or adverse modification of critical habitat.

Section 9 of the ESA broadly prohibits the taking of any listed species of fish or wildlife by "any person."[9] Both federal and nonfederal (i.e., private and state) actions are within the statutory prohibition. The statute defines *take* as "to harass, harm, pursue, hunt, shoot, wound, kill, trap, capture, or collect, or to attempt to engage in any such conduct."[10] The Supreme Court's *Sweet Home* decision upheld the FWS's regulatory interpretation of Section 9 to apply the take prohibition to significant habitat modification activities on nonfederal land.[11] The Section 9 protections for listed plants are distinct and incorporate state plant protection law requirements. Section 9 makes it unlawful for any person to "remove and reduce to possession" any listed plant from federal land areas, or to "maliciously damage or destroy any such species on any such area."[12] That section also prohibits any person to "remove, cut, dig up, or damage or destroy any [listed plant] species on any other area in knowing violation of any law or regulation of any State or in the course of any violation of a State criminal trespass law."[13]

The service may issue a permit under ESA Section 10(a) to authorize the "incidental take" of protected species. An incidental taking is one that is "incidental to, and not the purpose of, the carrying out of an otherwise lawful activity."[14] Similarly, for activities subject to the federal consultation requirement of Section 7, the biological opinion may include an incidental take statement authorizing such incidental take where it will not jeopardize the species' continued existence.[15] The statement must include reasonable and prudent measures that the service deems necessary or appropriate to minimize the impact of any incidental take on the species.[16]

Two provisions of the ESA are of special interest for the act's developing application to habitat and ecosystem conservation purposes. First, Section 2(b) provides that one purpose of the act is to "provide a means whereby the ecosystems upon which listed species depend may be conserved."[17] Second, Section 7(a)(1) directs all federal agencies to use their authorities to further the purposes of the ESA by carrying out programs for the conservation of listed species.[18] Although conserving the ecosystems upon which endangered species depend is one of the identified purposes of the ESA, no specific ESA program exists to implement this purpose.[19] The critical habitat provisions of the ESA are not coterminous with an ecosystem conservation approach because critical habitat often is not designated for listed species.[20] Also, the critical habitat designation and protections focus only on the essential elements of the habitat for the listed species and not all of the ecosystem functions of that habitat.

Nevertheless, despite the absence of a specific ESA program for ecosystem conservation, at least one federal court has indicated that the Section 2(b) purposes and Section 7(a)(1) obligations form the basis for a required ecosystem management approach. In *Seattle Audubon Society v. Lyons*,[21] Judge Dwyer upheld the president's Forest Plan for the Pacific Northwest old growth forests in the range of the northern spotted owl, and stated that the Bureau of Land Management and the Forest Service *had* to plan on an ecosystem basis to address forest conditions in that area. Thus, the ESA at times can be "a surrogate law for ecosystems."[22]

SHIFTING FOCUS OF THE ESA
FROM INDIVIDUAL SPECIES
TO HABITAT CONSERVATION

A series of judicial decisions through the 1980s and 1990s highlights the changing role of the ESA. The ESA has evolved from a program focusing on individual species and specific projects and proposals to its present application integrating endangered species impact and habitat conservation evaluations into programmatic decisions made at the regional or ecosystem level. *Cabinet Mountains Wilderness/Scotchman's Peak Grizzly Bears v. Peterson* [23] provides an example of the initial form of ESA litigation. In that case, environmental interests challenged the FWS biological opinion for a proposal to conduct exploratory drilling for copper and silver deposits in the Cabinet Mountains wilderness area in northwestern Montana. The FWS biological opinion concluded that the drilling was likely to jeopardize the threatened grizzly bear, but it included alternative measures to "completely compensate" for the adverse effects on the grizzly bear population. Based on these alternative measures, the Forest Service concluded that the impacts of the drilling program would ensure that the bears' continued existence was not threatened nor its critical habitat adversely modified. The District of Columbia Circuit Court of Appeals upheld the Forest Service's action, finding that sufficient evidence existed to support the agency's determination that the drilling proposal would not endanger the grizzly bear population.

Next, in *Thomas v. Peterson*, [24] the Ninth Circuit ruled that the Forest Service violated the ESA when it failed to prepare a biological assessment to determine whether construction of the Jersey Jack Road in the Nez Perce National Forest in Idaho might affect the endangered Rocky Mountain gray wolf. The court concluded that this ESA violation must be remedied by an injunction of the road-building project pending ESA compliance. [25] The Ninth Circuit also rejected the Forest Service request that the court make a finding that the project was not likely to affect the threatened wolf, noting that Congress had assigned that determination to FWS and had prescribed specific procedures for the evaluation. [26]

Later ESA cases began to review natural resource management projects on a broader scale with more wide-ranging implications. In a challenge to Forest Service timber management practices in the East Texas National

Forests, environmental interests established that even-aged timber management violated Section 7 because the Forest Service had not taken the steps necessary to ensure its activities did not jeopardize the continued existence of the red-cockaded woodpecker.[27] The court also concluded that the timber management practices resulted in "harm," giving rise to a Section 9 taking based on a severe decline in the woodpecker population over ten years resulting from significant habitat modification on Forest Service lands.[28] The district court enjoined these violations and required reconsultation with FWS.[29]

The programmatic reach of ESA restrictions achieved new levels in the Pacific Northwest with the northern spotted owl cases. This litigation has forced the federal government to take action at each of the key stages of the ESA process, listing and critical habitat designation under Section 4 and consultation on regional management plans under Section 7.[30] For instance, in *Lane County Audubon Society v. Jamison,*[31] the court enjoined future timber sales on Bureau of Land Management forest land until BLM consulted with FWS under Section 7 on the "Jamison Strategy," the agency's management guidelines for the conservation of the northern spotted owl. The Ninth Circuit held that the Jamison Strategy itself was an agency action because it developed a "detailed management strategy" that established total annual allowable harvest from BLM forest lands in northern spotted owl habitat. Until consultation occurred on the strategy and the underlying plans for BLM timber sales, new sales were enjoined from proceeding.

After certain stocks of Snake River salmon were listed as threatened or endangered in 1991 and 1992, litigation over potential effects on these species from resource management activities helped further define the habitat conservation application of the ESA. A key point for this expansion was the *Pacific Rivers Council v. Thomas* litigation that brought in two similar lawsuits, one in Oregon[32] and one in Idaho.[33] The cases alleged that the Forest Service had violated Section 7 of the ESA by failing to consult with the NMFS regarding the effect of various national forest management plans on listed Snake River salmon. In the Oregon case, the district court held that the two forest plans at issue were agency "actions" requiring consultation under ESA Section 7, and that the Forest Service watershed or site-specific consultation approach with NMFS was inadequate to satisfy the forest-plan-level consultation obligation.[34] The court also enjoined the Forest Service from undertaking additional timber, range, or road-building projects pending full compliance with the ESA consultation requirements. On appeal, the Ninth Circuit upheld the initial injunction and also reversed and remanded the portion of the district court's order excluding ongoing and announced timber, range, and road projects from the injunction, pending ESA compliance by the Forest Service.[35]

Prior to the Ninth Circuit decision, the plaintiffs had filed a similar action in Idaho. After the Ninth Circuit ruling, the Pacific Rivers Council moved for a preliminary injunction based on that precedent. In January 1995, the Idaho district court enjoined all ongoing, announced, and proposed logging, grazing, mining, and road-building activities that might affect endangered Snake River salmon on six Idaho national forests.[36] Faced with the actual or pending shutdown of numerous operations across these eight Oregon and Idaho forests, the Forest Service, resource development interests, and local communities were forced into a state of urgent response. Ultimately, within ten days of the entry of the Idaho injunction, a stay of the injunction was agreed to between the plaintiffs and the government after the plaintiffs received assurances from the Forest Service that it and NMFS would complete the required Section 7 consultations within an expedited forty-five-day time frame. Because of the stay, no forest activities were actually forced to shut down. Nevertheless, the injunction order demonstrated the powerful reach of the ESA consultation requirements to disrupt resource management activities in the national forests.

The salmon issues in the national forests of the inland Pacific Northwest have led the Forest Service to expand Endangered Species Act–based management requirements beyond listed species to consider all species of anadromous and nonanadromous native fish and habitat. The agency has now gone far beyond the basic ESA requirements of ensuring the continued existence of listed species and preventing adverse modification or destruction of critical habitat. Instead, the Forest Service is now implementing an amplified view of the Endangered Species Act to conserve aquatic ecosystems and related species on federal forest lands. This situation demonstrates the current expansive impact of the ESA as an ecosystem conservation law.

These cases highlight the judicial emphasis on certain aspects of the ESA that have combined in a powerful fashion in the litigation over endangered species habitat protection on federal lands in the Pacific Northwest. The cases emphasize that even broad planning decisions must be treated as agency "actions" requiring consultation under the ESA, that injunctive relief is generally available to allow the consultation process to function, and that species protection concerns will be incorporated into judicial review of challenged actions. As described below, the application of similar habitat conservation planning concerns to private projects and activities on private lands presents issues of both Section 9 ESA takings and potential governmental Fifth Amendment constitutional takings of private property.

WHAT ACTIVITIES CONSTITUTE A TAKE OF A PROTECTED SPECIES?

The *Sweet Home* decision upheld the Fish and Wildlife Service's "harm" regulation against a broad challenge to all possible applications of the regulation to habitat-altering activities. The decision thus leaves for later case-by-case resolution the "difficult questions of proximity and degree" of determining what circumstances establish a prohibited Section 9 taking of protected wildlife.[37] Even prior to the *Sweet Home* decision, the lower courts were struggling with this question, and the Supreme Court's ruling appears for the time being to leave the determination of these matters for the lower courts without much guidance on the specific application of the ESA Section 9 take prohibition to habitat-altering activities.

Prior to *Sweet Home,* the Ninth Circuit had indicated that the FWS's inclusion of habitat modification within the "harm" regulation followed the plain language of the statute and was consistent with the act's legislative history. In *Palila v. Hawaii Dep't. Land and Natural Resources,*[38] the Ninth Circuit upheld the district court's determination that the State of Hawaii's maintenance of feral goats and sheep in the Palila bird's critical habitat constituted an unlawful ESA taking. In that case, the State of Hawaii argued that the district court had construed the FWS's harm definition too broadly, but Hawaii did not directly challenge the harm regulation as beyond the scope of the FWS's discretion to promulgate. The Ninth Circuit concluded that the district court properly construed the harm regulation. In doing so, the Ninth Circuit reviewed whether the regulation was reasonable and consistent with congressional intent to ascertain if the district court's interpretation of the regulation was consistent with the FWS's construction of the statute.

Other decisions construing the harm regulation have focused primarily on how harm to a listed species might be established through habitat modification. These cases generally address the quantum of proof required to establish a taking through habitat modification, and do not address whether the FWS permissibly could treat habitat modification as giving rise to a taking. For instance, in *Sierra Club v. Yeutter*,[39] the appellate court upheld the district court's determination that Forest Service even-aged management practices in red-cockaded woodpecker habitat in Texas National Forests resulted in harm to the species, giving rise to a Section 9 take. The district court had concluded that a severe decline in the woodpecker population over ten years resulting from the Forest Service's significant habitat modification was sufficient to establish harm. This overall population decline was adequate proof since "'[h]arm' does not necessarily require the proof of the death of specific or individual members of the species."[40]

Next, in a Section 9 challenge to Forest Service road-building activities and the resultant impact on listed grizzly bears caused by forest road densities, the reviewing district court concluded that the "pivotal element of Plaintiffs' claim is a showing of injury to the listed species."[41] However, the court held that scientific evidence supporting the conclusion that current road densities were interfering with essential behavioral patterns was insufficient to demonstrate harm without the additional showing that "the degree of impairment is so significant that it is actually killing or injuring grizzly bears." In *Morrill v. Lujan*,[42] the court held that the modification or degradation of suitable habitat for the Perdido Key beach mouse was insufficient to establish a Section 9 taking without establishing the link between habitat modification and injury to the species. Similarly, in *American Bald Eagle v. Bhatti*,[43] the appellate court ruled that there must be an actual injury to the listed species for there to be harm under the ESA. The challengers failed in *Bhatti* to show harm to bald eagles arising from use of lead slugs in deer hunting, and the court rejected the option of establishing a risk-based approach to determining a Section 9 taking.

A series of recent Ninth Circuit cases continues this line of analysis and emphasizes the degree of proof and causation required to establish a prohibited Section 9 taking arising from habitat-altering activities. In *National Wildlife Federation v. Burlington Northern Railroad, Inc.*,[44] the court held there must be a sufficient likelihood of future harm to obtain relief under ESA Section 9. To establish a taking, a plaintiff must show actual significant impairment of a species' breeding or feeding habits *and* prove that the alleged habitat degradation prevents recovery of the species. Thus, there was no actionable Section 9 taking from the railroad's failure to take further measures (such as reducing train speeds, equipping trains with air bags or other protective devices for train/bear collisions, and obtaining an incidental take permit) to address a corn spill on its tracks where the immediate potential harm to listed grizzly bears had passed. Also, the habitat impact was localized and did not significantly affect the grizzlies' feeding behavior.

Next, in *Forest Conservation Council v. Rosboro Lumber Co.*,[45] the court ruled that to establish a Section 9 taking, a plaintiff has the burden of demonstrating that harm to a listed species will, to a reasonable certainty, result from the defendant's habitat-altering activities. The mere possibility that these actions could cause harm to a listed species is insufficient. Lastly, in *Marbled Murrelet v. Babbitt*,[46] decided after *Sweet Home,* the court upheld the district court's injunction against a private company's timber harvest operations on its own lands that would have significantly modified the habitat of the listed seabird in northern California old-growth forests. The court specifically rejected the lumber company's contention that *Sweet Home* indicates that harm to a species must already have occurred before injunctive relief is warranted. Instead, the Ninth Circuit reiterated its conclusion from *Rosboro* that "a showing of *future injury* to an endangered or threatened species is actionable under the ESA."[47] In the *Marbled Murrelet* case, the appellate court concluded that the plaintiffs had presented sufficient evidence to support the district court's conclusion that "there was a reasonable certainty of imminent harm to [the birds] from Pacific Lumber's intended logging operation."[48]

In sum, these cases emphasize that despite the broad pronouncement of *Sweet Home,* the individualized inquiries into the proof and causation established by the specific facts of each case will continue to control what habitat-altering actions will be considered Section 9 takings. In turn, this requirement for fact-specific inquiry and proof may, as discussed below, limit the range of instances when an ESA regulation concerning habitat protection to avoid or minimize a Section 9 taking will result in a governmental taking of private property.

ESA TAKINGS AND CONSTITUTIONAL TAKINGS

The broad reach of the developing ESA habitat-protection focus and the application of the Section 9 take prohibition to habitat-altering activities on private lands raises the Fifth Amendment constitutional takings issue.[49] Perhaps recognizing this possibility, each of the principal ESA reform or reauthorization bills introduced in the 104th Congress addressed the constitutional takings issue in some manner. These proposals range from prohibiting government action under the ESA that results in more than a 20 percent diminution in value of nonfederal property unless compensation is offered, to creating a statutory entitlement to fair-market-value compensation for ESA-regulation-imposed declines in property value (without barring such agency action) or simply preserving constitutional claims for a taking for ESA requirements imposed after an owner purchases private property.[50] (See Chapter 6 for more discussion of proposed reauthorization legislation.)

Recent judicial developments, including the Supreme Court decisions in *Lucas v. South Carolina Coastal Council*[51] and *Dolan v. City of Tigard*,[52] have increased the potential for successful Fifth Amendment takings cases arising from government regulation of private property. The Fifth Amendment to the federal Constitution provides that private property shall not "be taken for public use, without just compensation."[53] While the regulatory takings area continues in a state of transition, these recent developments suggest the federal courts' receptivity to takings claims arising from environmental regulations, possibly including ESA regulatory activities. For instance, courts have found regulatory takings arising from a wetlands permit denial,[54] enactment of the Surface Mining and Reclamation Act,[55] and the installation of groundwater monitoring wells near a Superfund site.[56]

CONSTITUTIONAL TAKINGS PRINCIPLES

Background Takings Principles

The Supreme Court's takings decisions have generally applied one of two tests to ascertain whether a compensable taking exists. In *Penn Central Transportation Co. v. City of New York*,[57] the Court examined three factors to determine whether a government regulation comprises a taking: the character of the governmental action, its economic impact, and its interference with reasonable investment-backed expectations. Subsequently, in *Agins v. Tiburon*,[58] the Court stated that a law would effect a taking if it "does not substantially advance legitimate state interests or denies an owner economically viable use of his land."[59] Although there is some overlap between these two tests, the more recent decisions suggest a trend toward application of *Agins*'s two-part standard.[60]

An important issue is the level of governmental action necessary to trigger a taking. For example, restrictions on a land-use activity may flow from development conditions imposed as permit conditions, mitigation requirements, or from a permit denial. In *United States v. Riverside Bayview Homes*,[61] the Supreme Court suggested that "[o]nly when a permit is denied and the effect of the denial is to prevent 'economically viable' use of the land in question can it be said that a taking has occurred."[62] Under this approach, as in *Penn Central,* mere regulation of natural resource or land development projects, such as through permit conditions, would not give rise to a taking so long as economically viable uses of the property remain. However, the Court has since held that government regulation could give rise to a compensable temporary taking for losses resulting from the deprivation of the use of property during the time a regulatory taking is imposed.[63] Also, in *Dolan,* a building permit condition was held to be a compensable regulatory taking.[64] Thus, permit conditions or regulations, short of an outright permit denial, may give rise to a takings claim if they preclude certain economically viable development alternatives.

The Lucas *Decision*

The *Lucas* case involved the South Carolina Beachfront Management Act, which (to prevent beach erosion and protect the coastal dune systems of the barrier islands) prohibited the development of habitable improvements seaward of a baseline representing the inlandmost point of erosion during the past forty years. The Court accepted the state trial court's determination that the act deprived Lucas of all economically viable use of his land.[65] Based on this assumption, the Court developed a categorical rule that such total regulatory takings must be compensated unless the use restriction has a foundation in a state's common law of property or nuisance in effect when a landowner acquired the parcel. Regulations that "leave the owner of land without economically beneficial or productive options for its use—typically, as here, by requiring land to be left substantially in its natural state—carry with them a heightened risk that private property is being pressed into some form of public service under the guise of mitigating serious public harm."[66]

If state property or nuisance law holds that the regulated activity was a nuisance for which abatement could be sought or was a use inconsistent with the property owner's title interest in the land, the regulation will not give rise to a taking. Determining whether underlying state law previously regulated the activity will ordinarily require an analysis of (1) the degree of harm to public lands and resources or adjacent private property posed by the proposed development; (2) the social value of the proposed action and its suitability to the environment in question; and (3) the relative ease with which the alleged harm can be avoided by measures taken by the developer and the government or adjacent private landowners.[67]

The Dolan *Decision*

In *Dolan v. City of Tigard,*[68] the Court addressed the required relationship between permit conditions and projected impacts of proposed development to determine whether a taking occurred. In *Dolan,* a landowner sought a permit to redevelop her 1.67-acre commercial property partly located within the one-hundred-year floodplain along Fanno Creek in Tigard, Oregon. The applicable city ordinance and comprehensive plan required the landowner to dedicate a portion of her property within the floodplain for storm drain improvements, and also required the dedication of a fifteen-foot strip of land as a pedestrian/bicycle pathway along the creek.

The Court framed the issue as a two-part inquiry. First, based on its earlier decision in *Nollan v. California Coastal Commission,*[69] does the "essential nexus" exist between the "legitimate state interest" and the permit condition exacted by the government?[70] Second, is there a "rough proportionality" between the required exaction and the proposed project? No precise mathematical calculation is required, but the regulatory entity must make some sort of individualized determination that the required dedication is related in both nature and extent to the impact of the proposed development.

Applying this standard, the Court found first that the essential nexus was present for both permit conditions, the floodplain dedication and the greenway. But while the floodplain dedication for storm sewer improvements survived the second prong of the standard, the greenway dedication did not. The city never stated how a public greenway was required for its flood-control purposes, and this requirement resulted in Dolan's loss of her ability to exclude others from her property. According to Chief Justice Rehnquist, "[i]t is difficult to see why recreational visitors trampling along petitioner's floodplain easement are sufficiently related to the city's legitimate interest in reducing floodplain problems along Fanno Creek, and the city has not attempted to make any individualized determination to support this part of its request."[71] Thus, in a 5-4 decision, the Court held the required greenway dedication to be a compensable taking.

ESA REGULATORY ACTION AS A GOVERNMENTAL TAKING

Despite the political discourse that has linked the constitutional takings/ private property rights debates, there has been little litigation addressing the subject under the ESA. In *Christy v. Hodel,*[72] a Montana sheep grower challenged the ESA and regulations forbidding the taking of grizzly bears except under certain circumstances. The grower's sheep grazed on land leased from the Blackfoot tribe. In July 1982 the sheep herd was attacked by grizzly bears on a regular basis. Before the month was out, Christy lost eighty-four sheep to the grizzly bears, but Christy had killed one of the ESA-listed bears while protecting his flock. When the government fined Christy $3,000 for killing a protected species, Christy (together with other sheep growers) decided to sue the government, claiming among other things that by protecting grizzly bears, the Department of the Interior had transformed the bears into "governmental agents" who had physically taken his property. In denying this constitutional taking claim, the court held that the regulations complained of did not take, or even regulate the use of, Christy's sheep. Furthermore, the actions of the grizzly bears could not be attributed to the government, and "the losses sustained by the [sheep grower] are the incidental, and by no means inevitable, result of a reasonable regulation in the public interest."[73] Thus, there was no taking claim for the actions of the depredating bears since the government was "not answerable for the conduct of the bears."[74]

In *United States v. Kepler,*[75] Kepler made an agreement with an undercover Interior Department agent to transport a leopard and a cougar to Kentucky from Florida. When Kepler arrived in Kentucky, he was arrested and charged with two violations of Kentucky law, which prohibited the transportation of a leopard and cougar in interstate commerce without obtaining a written permit. He was also charged with transporting in interstate commerce a leopard in violation of the Endangered Species Act. The Department of the Interior seized the animals. Kepler alleged that the

ESA deprived him of the use of his property because his animals were seized. The Sixth Circuit held that the ESA does not effect an unconstitutional taking because the act does not prevent all sales of endangered wildlife, but only those sales in interstate or foreign commerce. Thus, Kepler presumably could have sold the animals within Florida without violating the ESA. The court also noted that the act allows the transportation or sale of endangered species if the secretary of the interior approves it for "scientific purposes or to enhance the propagation or survival of the affected species." Based on these provisions, the court found the act did not result in a taking.

These two ESA cases are of limited value in evaluating the potential for successful takings claims by private property owners following the *Sweet Home* decision and the Supreme Court's takings pronouncements in *Lucas* and *Dolan*. Importantly, the *Christy* and *Kepler* cases did not involve land-use issues, but instead concerned the losses of individual animals that were alleged to be an unconstitutional deprivation of private property. As the *Dolan* and *Nollan* cases illustrate, the courts are generally more receptive to constitutional takings claims that involve some physical invasion of the claimant's right to use his or her own land, such as the greenway easement in *Dolan* or the beachfront access easement in *Nollan*. Also, as in *Lucas*, a regulation that results in the total denial of all economically viable use of private property will generally be considered to work a Fifth Amendment taking.

Two cases from the federal wetlands permitting context demonstrate the application of these principles. The wetlands permitting examples may be better predictors for claims of regulatory takings based on ESA requirements, since the wetlands context similarly involves land-use restrictions imposed in the name of public natural resource protection. Also, the wetlands permitting requirement provides a direct analog to the ESA Section 10 incidental take permit process or the Section 7 biological opinion process for private property use or development involving some federal approval or assistance.

In *Loveladies Harbor, Inc. v. United States*,[76] the Federal Circuit Court of Appeals held that denial of a Clean Water Act Section 404 wetlands permit by the Army Corps of Engineers for a 12.5-acre development in New Jersey resulted in a compensable taking. The appellate court stated the issue as whether "when the Government fulfills its obligations to preserve and protect the public interest, may the cost of obtaining that public benefit fall solely upon the affected property owner, or is it to be shared

by the community at large?" The Federal Circuit determined that the wetland permit denial deprived the landowner of all economically viable use
of its land, and it upheld the compensation award of $2.6 million by the
Court of Federal Claims.

By contrast, in *Florida Rock Industries v. United States*,[77] the Federal Circuit overturned a trial court decision finding a taking from the denial of a
wetlands permit for a limestone mining operation. The decision was remanded "for determination of what economic use as measured by market
value, if any, remained after the permit denial, and . . . whether, in light
of the properly assessed value" the plaintiff had a valid takings claim.[78] If,
upon remand, there is some (but not a total) reduction in overall market
value of the property, the inquiry must focus on whether that partial reduction rises to the level of taking or is instead the result of permissible
government regulation, based on application of general takings principles, such as the *Penn Central* and *Agins* tests.[79]

The cases discussed above demonstrate the likely need for some type
of physical invasion of private property or a regulation that denies an
owner of all economically viable use of his or her land (or at least all
economically viable use of some distinctly identified portion of the owner's
land) to give rise to an unconstitutional taking for ESA-imposed restrictions for land-use or habitat conservation. Significantly, the *Christy* case
supports the proposition that actions of the protected wildlife itself (grizzly bears in that instance) would not be considered a "physical invasion."
This conclusion is consistent with the general premise of state wildlife law
that all wildlife is owned by the state and managed for the public's benefit.[80] Thus, under the *Lucas* framework, private landowners take their title
to property subject to this extant state-law recognition of wildlife's access
to and use of existing habitat on that property. For example, an early
Massachusetts decision recognized the public's right to have rivers kept
open and free for anadromous fish such as salmon "to pass from the sea,
through such rivers, to the ponds and headwaters, to cast their spawn."[81]

Nevertheless, the government's own physical invasion or regulation of
private property under the guise of the ESA (other than through the mere
use of private property by wildlife) could still give rise to a compensable
taking under certain circumstances. Certainly, the lesson of *Sweet Home* is
that private-property-related activities may be regulated under the Section
9 take prohibition or the Section 7 consultation requirement and jeopardy
prohibition. Section 9 could be (and has been) applied directly to prohibit
a broad array of habitat-related activities: the clearing of nesting habitat

for endangered birds such as the California gnatcatcher or the golden-cheeked warbler in anticipation of real estate development; the harvesting of timber used as nesting habitat by species such as the northern spotted owl, marbled murrelet, or red-cockaded woodpecker; and the draining of ponds and wetlands utilized by the San Marcos salamander. The Section 9 prohibition has also been applied to enjoin an irrigation district from pumping water from the Sacramento River where that pumping killed listed winter-run chinook salmon.[82]

Although the Section 7 consultation requirement and jeopardy prohibition do not apply directly to private interests, if a federal permit or approval is required for private action, the prohibition or restriction of the desired action might give rise to a constitutional takings claim. For example, restrictions imposed under Section 7 consultations have limited the amount of water available to irrigators under federal reclamation contracts,[83] and required mining operators working claims on a mix of private and federal land to close roads and develop an anadromous fish habitat protection plan as a condition of project approval. Also, if a permit were required under Section 404 of the Clean Water Act to allow a landowner to fill wetlands on private property for the purpose of residential or other development, the denial of that permit as a result of a jeopardy determination following an ESA Section 7 consultation could prohibit the desired use of the property. As another example, if Section 7 precluded the BLM from authorizing groundwater dewatering activities on public lands necessary to allow mining of or access to patented or unpatented minerals and mining claims, because such dewatering potentially could affect the surface water habitat for a listed species, a taking of that property interest might ensue. Under these and similar conditions, the level of regulation imposed might, depending on the specific facts and circumstances presented, give rise to a prohibited taking of private property.

The specific requirements of the ESA permitting and consultation processes under Section 10 and Section 7 help identify when specific regulatory activities might give rise to a compensable taking of private property. Under the Section 10(a) incidental take permit requirements, the issuance of the permit must be supported by a habitat conservation plan specifying, among other things, what impact will likely result from the proposed incidental taking, what steps the permit applicant will take to minimize and mitigate these impacts, the availability of funding for plan implementation, and the procedures to address unforeseen circumstances.[84] In approving an incidental take permit, the FWS must find that the applicant will, to the maximum extent practicable, minimize and mitigate the impacts of the incidental taking.[85]

In the Section 7 federal agency consultation process, the consultation regulations contain built-in limitations on the scope of regulatory action available for the FWS to suggest reasonable and prudent measures to minimize the incidental take of a listed species, and also limitations on reasonable and prudent alternatives that may be suggested to avoid jeopardizing the continued existence of a listed species or to avoid the destruction or adverse modification of critical habitat. Reasonable and prudent alternatives must be consistent with the intended purpose of the original project, must be consistent with the scope of the federal agency's legal authority, and must be "economically and technologically feasible."[86] These restrictions indicate that requirements that, for instance, go so far as to deny a private project applicant all economically viable use of his or her property would not be an "economically feasible" reasonable and prudent alternative under the regulations. Similarly, reasonable and prudent measures intended to minimize incidental take "cannot alter the basic design, location, scope, duration, or timing of the [project] and may involve only minor changes."[87] While reasonable and prudent measures are intended to minimize the level of incidental take, "Congress also intended that the action go forward essentially as planned."[88] Thus, "[s]ubstantial design and routing changes . . . are inappropriate in the context of incidental take statements because the action already complies with Section 7(a)(2)" by avoiding jeopardy.[89]

Because of these inherent checks on the scope of ESA regulatory actions under Sections 7 and 10, it may be unlikely to reach the situation in which ESA restrictions would totally deprive an owner of all economically viable use of private land, or result in the physical invasion of private property so as to result in a compensable Fifth Amendment taking. In the ESA permitting and approval context, the "rough proportionality" test applied in *Dolan* suggests an additional check on the scope of ESA regulatory measures to prevent them from rising to a level of an uncompensated taking of private property. For instance, if a habitat conservation plan to be approved by the FWS as part of a Section 10 incidental take permit requires specific mitigation measures (such as the dedication of certain lands to wildlife habitat purposes to compensate for developments to other areas), the *Dolan* standard indicates that these measures must be based on an individualized determination that the scope of required mitigation is related both in nature and extent to the impact of the plan development. The *Dolan* standard thus suggests that the FWS may be required to undertake a somewhat more specific inquiry than it may have been doing previously to link specific mitigation measures and permit requirements to identified development or land-use impacts.

To the extent individual Section 10 permit and Section 7 consultation analyses already incorporate such determinations, the *Dolan* standard indicates no compensable taking of private property should occur, absent a total denial of all economically viable use of a private landowner's property. Overall, based on the inherent limitations on the scope of reasonable and prudent alternatives and measures the FWS can impose under the Section 7 consultation regulations, and considering the individualized permit decisions already made under the Section 10 incidental take permit regulations, the instances in which ESA regulation of habitat-modifying activities on private land may give rise to a compensable taking should be somewhat rare. However, as in the *Loveladies Harbor* example from the wetlands context, the case of an outright permit denial or jeopardy determination that precludes all economically viable use of private property may present those circumstances in which a compensable taking is present.

CONCLUSIONS

The majority of concerns over the scope of ESA regulation of habitat-altering activities on nonfederal lands will likely be decided in determinations about what actions constitute a prohibited taking of a listed species under Section 9, and what are the standards of proof required to demonstrate whether such a taking has occurred or will occur in the future. As forecast by Justice Stevens in *Sweet Home,* it is in this case-by-case resolution of the act's broad provisions that the scope of its habitat protection requirement will be spelled out in individual instances. While the possibility of some conflict with the desires of private property owners remains in this case-by-case approach, the limitations inherent in the act, together with the outer limits of permissible government regulation as illustrated by the constitutional takings cases including *Dolan,* should help limit the potential for extreme adverse effects on private property use and development. For these existing limitations to function properly, the ESA's present regulations and consultation standards must be conscientiously applied by federal agencies, species protection advocates, and private property owners. Doing so should help avoid the *Sweet Home* dissent's concerns, written by Justice Scalia, that the decision "imposes unfairness to the point of financial ruin . . . [for even] the simplest farmer who finds his land conscripted to national zoological use."

NOTES

The authors gratefully acknowledge the efforts of attorney Paula A. Fleck, Holland and Hart, in the research and preparation of this article. An earlier version of this article appeared in *Environmental Law Reporter,* 1996, volume 26.

1   The Supreme Court held on 19 March 1997, that resource development interests as well as those persons who allege an interest in the preservation of endangered species may fall within the zone of interest protected by the ESA and have standing to sue under the statute (*Bennett v. Spear,* No. 95-813, 1997 WS 119566 [19 Mar. 1997]). The Supreme Court also addressed ESA standing issues in *Lujan v. Defenders of Wildlife,* 504 U.S. 555 (1992), where it held that wildlife and conservation organization plaintiffs failed to demonstrate the requisite injury in fact to challenge a rule interpreting ESA Section 7 to apply only within the United States and on the high seas.

2   437 U.S. 153 (1978).

3   115 S. Ct. 2407, 2418 (1995).

4   16 U.S.C. § 1533.

5   In general, the FWS is responsible for terrestrial and freshwater species. The NMFS is responsible for marine species, including anadromous fish such as salmon and steelhead trout that hatch in fresh water, spend most of their adult life in the ocean, and then return to fresh water to spawn. See 50 C.F.R. §§ 17.2(b), 402.01(b).

6   50 C.F.R. § 402.02.

7   50 C.F.R. § 402.14(a).

8   See ibid. § 402.14(h)(3).

9   16 U.S.C. § 1538(a)(1). The statutory prohibition applies only to endangered species, but has been extended to threatened species by regulation 50 C.F.R. § 17.31(a).

10   16 U.S.C. § 1532(19).

11   *Babbitt v. Sweet Home Chapter of Communities for a Great Oregon,* 115 S. Ct. 2407, 2418 (1995). In *Sweet Home,* private property owners and logging companies dependent on the forest products industries challenged the statutory validity of the FWS regulation defining "harm" to include habitat-modification activities that actually kill or injure wildlife. The challengers argued that Congress did not intend for the word *take* to include habitat modification. The Court found support for the FWS definition in the statutory language and legislative history. The Court also noted that the act authorizes the issuance of permits for the unintended, incidental "take" of an endangered species as a result of an otherwise lawful activity. Congress's inclusion of this provision in the act

supported the secretary's conclusion that activities not directly intended to harm an endangered species, such as habitat modification from land-use development or natural resource extraction activities, may result in an unlawful indirect taking unless the FWS or NMFS authorize the taking.

12   16 U.S.C. § 1538(a)(2)(B).

13   Ibid.

14   16 U.S.C. § 1539(a)(1)(B).

15   50 C.F.R. § 402.14(i).

16   Ibid.

17   16 U.S.C. § 1531(b). The Supreme Court noted in *Sweet Home* that this ecosystem conservation purpose is one of the "central purposes" of the ESA (*Sweet Home*, 115 S. Ct. at 2413).

18   16 U.S.C. § 1536(a)(1).

19   See, for example, National Research Council, *Science and the Endangered Species Act* (Washington, D.C.: National Academy Press, 1995), p. 179, noting that while "ecosystem protection is of paramount importance to the overall preservation of species," the ESA focuses on listing species, and any policy for implementing ecosystem protection is "untested."

20   Ibid., p. 76, "That nearly 80% of all species listed do not have critical habitat designations is a cause for concern."

21   871 F. Supp. 1291, 1311 (W.D. Wash. 1994), affirmed on other grounds sub nom. *Seattle Audubon Soc'y. v. Moseley*, 80 F.3d 1401 (9th Cir. 1996).

22   O. A. Houck, Nature, Nurture and Property Rights, *The Economist* July 1995, 24–25.

23   685 F.2d 678 (D.C. Cir. 1982).

24   753 F.2d 754 (9th Cir. 1985).

25   Ibid. at 764 (citing *TVA v. Hill*, 437 U.S. 153 [1978]).

26   753 F.2d at 765.

27   *Sierra Club v. Lyng*, 694 F. Supp. 1260 (E.D. Tex. 1988), affirmed in part, vacated in part, *Sierra Club v. Yeutter*, 926 F.2d 429, 439 (5th Cir. 1991).

28   *Sierra Club v. Yeutter*, 926 F.2d at 437–439.

29   Ibid. at 440.

30   See generally M. Bonnett and K. Zimmerman, Politics and Presentation: The Endangered Species Act and the Northern Spotted Owl, *Ecology Law Quarterly* 1991:105.

31   958 F.2d 290 (9th Cir. 1992).

32   *Pacific Rivers Council v. Robertson*, 854 F. Supp. 713 (D. Or. 1993), affirmed in part, reversed in part sub nom. *Pacific Rivers Council v. Thomas*, 30 F.3d 1050 (9th Cir. 1994), cert. denied, 115 S. Ct. 1793 (1995).

33   *Pacific Rivers Council v. Thomas*, 873 F. Supp. 365 (D. Idaho 1995), appeal dismissed as moot, Nos. 95-35068, -35171, -35208 (9th Cir. 10 July 1995).

34   *Pacific Rivers Council v. Robertson*, 854 F. Supp. at 723.

35   *Pacific Rivers Council v. Thomas*, 30 F.3d at 1056.

36   *Pacific Rivers Council v. Thomas*, 873 F. Supp. at 370, 372.

37   See *Sweet Home*, 115 S. Ct. at 2418.

38   852 F.2d 1106, 1108 (9th Cir. 1988).

39   926 F.2d 429 (5th Cir. 1991).
40   *Sierra Club v. Lyng,* 694 F. Supp. 1260, 1270 (E.D. Tex. 1988) (citations omitted), affirmed 926 F.2d 429, 439 (5th Cir. 1991).
41   *Swan View Coalition, Inc. v. Turner,* 824 F. Supp. 923, 939 (D. Mont. 1992).
42   802 F. Supp. 424, 430 (S.D. Ala. 1992).
43   9 F.3d 163, 166 (1st Cir. 1993).
44   23 F.3d 1508, 1511 (9th Cir. 1994).
45   50 F.3d 781, 787–788 (9th Cir. 1995).
46   83 F.3d 1060 (9th Cir. 1996).
47   Ibid. at 1064–1065 (quoting *Rosboro,* 50 F.3d at 783); emphasis added.
48   Ibid. at 1067–1068. The evidence presented showed that logging operations in the marbled murrelet's habitat would likely harm the birds by impairing their breeding (e.g., by substantially reducing nesting opportunities and habitat), and by increasing the likelihood of attack by predators such as stellar jays because of more open and fragmented forest stands resulting from logging. See *Marbled Murrelet v. Pacific Lumber Co.,* 880 F. Supp. 1343, 1366 (N.D. Cal. 1995), affirmed sub nom. *Marbled Murrelet v. Babbitt,* 80 F.3d 1060 (9th Cir. 1996).
49   The Fifth Amendment provides that private property shall not "be taken for public use, without just compensation" (U.S. Const., amend. 5).
50   See S. 1364, 104th Cong., 1st Sess. (1995); S. 768, 104th Cong., 1st Sess. (1995); H.R. 2275, 104th Cong., 1st Sess. (1995).
51   120 L. Ed. 2d 798 (1992).
52   129 L. Ed. 2d 304 (1994).
53   U.S. Constitution, amend. 5.
54   *Loveladies Harbor, Inc. v. United States,* 28 F.3d 1711 (Fed. Cir. 1994).
55   *Whitney Benefits, Inc. v. United States,* 926 F.2d 1169 (Fed. Cir.), cert. denied, 112 S. Ct. 406 (1991).
56   *Hendler v. United States,* 952 F.2d 1364 (Fed. Cir. 1991).
57   438 U.S. 104 (1978).
58   447 U.S. 255 (1980).
59   Ibid. at 260 (citations omitted).
60   E.g., *Lucas,* 120 L. Ed. 2d at 813, 818.
61   474 U.S. 121 (1985).
62   474 U.S. at 127.
63   *First Evangelical Lutheran Church v. Los Angeles County,* 482 U.S. 304 (1987).
64   129 L. Ed. 2d at 322.
65   120 L. Ed. 2d at 815–816 & n.9.
66   *Lucas,* 120 L. Ed. 2d at 814.
67   120 L. Ed. 2d at 822.
68   129 L. Ed. 2d 304 (1994).
69   483 U.S. 825 (1987).
70   *Dolan,* 129 L. Ed. 2d at 317. In *Nollan,* the Court held that California's requirement for a lateral public easement across Nollan's beachfront property in exchange for a coastal area development approval was a taking because the condition was not sufficiently connected to the legitimate state purpose of preserving ocean views by regulating housing development (483 U.S. at 837).

71 *Dolan,* 129 L. Ed. 2d at 321.
72 857 F.2d 1324 (9th Cir. 1988).
73 857 F.2d at 1335.
74 Ibid.
75 531 F.2d 796 (6th Cir. 1976).
76 28 F.3d 1171 (Fed. Cir. 1994).
77 18 F.3d 1560, 1573 (Fed. Cir. 1994).
78 Ibid. at 1565.
79 Ibid. at 1568, 1570.
80 See, for example, Wyo. Stat. § 23-1-103; but see *Hughes v. Oklahoma,* 441 U.S.
    322 (1979) (terming state ownership concept a "legal fiction" and limiting its
    application to those regulatory measures that do not discriminate against inter-
    state commerce; thus, states can still promote wildlife conservation within their
    borders); and *Kleppe v. New Mexico,* 426 U.S. 529 (1976) ("Unquestionably the
    States have broad trustee and police powers over wild animals within their juris-
    diction. But . . . those powers exist only in so far as their exercise may be not
    incompatible with, or restrained by, the rights conveyed to the federal govern-
    ment by the constitution.") (citation and internal quotation omitted).
81 *Commonwealth v. Alger,* 7 Cush. 53, 98 (Mass. 1851).
82 *United States v. Glenn-Colusa Irrigation District,* 788 F. Supp. 1126, 1135 (E.D.
    Cal. 1995).
83 *O'Neill v. United States,* 50 F.3d 677, 680–682, 687 (9th Cir. 1995).
84 See 50 C.F.R. § 17.22(b)(1)(iii).
85 Ibid. § 17.22(b)(2).
86 50 C.F.R. § 402.02.
87 50 C.F.R. § 402.14(i)(2).
88 51 Fed. Reg. 19926, 19937 (3 June 1986).
89 Ibid. at 19937.

❊ 4 ❊

Biological Effectiveness
and Economic Impacts
of the Endangered Species Act

Jason F. Shogren and Patricia H. Hayward

INTRODUCTION

Markets serve society by organizing economic activity, and they use the prices of goods and services to communicate the wants and limits of a diverse society so as to coordinate economic decisions in the most efficient manner. The power of the market rests in its decentralized process of decision making and exchange; no central planner is needed to allocate resources. Optimal private decisions lead to optimal social outcomes.

But markets can fail to allocate environmental resources efficiently, often due to the inability of institutions to establish well-defined property rights for biological services. For endangered species and their habitats, markets will fail if prices do not communicate society's desires and constraints accurately. Prices either understate the full range of services provided by a species, or do not exist to send a signal to the marketplace about the social value of the asset. When individual decisions impose costs on or generate benefits for other individuals who are not fully compensated for losses or who do not fully pay for gains, a wedge is driven between what individuals want unilaterally and what society wants as a collective.

At the most basic level, the threat to endangered species exists because many of the services they provide are nonrival and nonexcludable. *Non-*

rival in this instance means that one person's use does not reduce another's use, and *nonexclusive* means that it is extremely costly to exclude others from the benefits or costs the service provides. For example, the life-support services provided to humanity from the diversity of species are provided to everyone.[1] As a result, endangered species with limited commercial or consumptive benefits, as reflected by market prices, are undervalued. In contrast, the commodity resources of the species or the habitat sheltering the species (e.g., chemicals, minerals, timber, game) are valued on the market, and the supply and demand reflect the relative scarcity of these goods. Therefore, there is pressure to harvest the commodity and consumptive services at the expense of the public services provided by endangered species.

The Endangered Species Act was enacted in 1973 to correct for the market failure associated with the unpriced social benefits of species and their habitats. The four basic conclusions of our evaluation of the biological effectiveness and economic impacts of the ESA are:

- There is no tangible objective way to measure biological effectiveness at this time.
- Even if there were an objective measure, the time span since passage of the ESA has been too short to establish any decisive conclusions on overall recovery of species.
- There is no national estimate of the transaction costs, opportunity costs of restricted property rights, and opportunity costs of public funds used in species recovery to the private property owners. The few regional studies that focus on a specific species suggest that distribution issues may be of more concern than efficiency questions, that is, the way the economic "pie" is split between people changes, but the size of the pie does not.
- There is no national estimate of the economic benefits, either private or social, of most of the approximately 1,125 listed species. Those species-by-species estimates of benefits that do exist are subject to numerous technical questions that could limit their usefulness for policy analysis.

BIOLOGICAL EFFECTIVENESS OF THE ESA

Since passage of the ESA, over 1,125 species of plants and animals in the United States have been listed as endangered or threatened. Is the ESA effective in protecting these and unlisted species in the United States? Answering this question involves answering several others first. For example, in evaluating the consequences of the ESA for native species, how should we define biological effectiveness? Is the ESA effective if it provides for the recovery of listed species to the point where they can be delisted? Is it effective if it helps reverse the trend in species abundance prior to recovery, or is the ESA effective if it simply prevents listed species from becoming extinct? A broad interpretation of effectiveness may also include an evaluation of the degree to which the ESA encourages management actions that prevent species from declining to the point of being considered for listing.

Beyond the various broad approaches to examining the biological effectiveness of the ESA, we must confront the issue of establishing a metric to measure effectiveness. What level of recovery is necessary to conclude that the act has been effective? For instance, how many species must have recovered and become delisted to make the judgment that the ESA has satisfactorily accomplished its goals? One? Five? A dozen? One hundred? Evaluating biological effectiveness is further complicated by the temporal scale of the extinction process and the difficulty of defining endpoints. Is twenty-three years long enough to judge the effectiveness of a law that begins working only after species have declined so far that they are in imminent danger of extinction? How long are we willing to give species to recover? In this brief review, we examine the biological effectiveness of the ESA from several perspectives. We also examine the constraints on assessing the biological effectiveness of a law that deals with a complex biological process that scientists have only begun to understand: species extinction.

First, we must realize that at present we really have no way to evaluate effectiveness because our evidence is only circumstantial. No controlled experiments have been conducted.[2] Keeping this limitation in mind, let us look at the effectiveness of the ESA in removing species from the threatened and endangered lists. Only a handful of species have achieved the goal of recovery. Among these are the eastern states' brown pelican (*Pelecanus occidentalis*), Utah's Rydberg milk-vetch (*Astragalus perianus*), and the California gray whale (*Eschrichtius robustus*). With so few species achieving recovery and so many continuing to exist in a tenuous state, it might appear that the ESA is clearly ineffective in achieving its goals. But is it? Before species can recover, they obviously must halt their slide toward extinction and then increase. If we use these criteria for our evaluation, the ESA begins to look better. A 1994 report to Congress listed the status of threatened and endangered species as follows: 42 percent stable or improving, 34 percent declining, 1 percent extinct, and 23 percent unknown.[3] Species downlisted from endangered to threatened include the Aleutian Canada goose (*Branta canadensis leucopareia*), greenback cutthroat trout (*Salmo clarki stomias*), Virginia round-leaf birch (*Betula uber*), and bald eagle (*Haliaeetus leucocephalus*). Of course, we have no way to evaluate how many species would be extinct today without the protection of the ESA. In 1995, the National Research Council concluded that "it is impossible to quantify the ESA's biological effects—i.e., how well it has prevented species from becoming extinct . . . [but] the ESA has successfully prevented some species from becoming extinct. Retention of the ESA would help prevent species extinction."[4]

Furthermore, Belovsky et al.[5] noted that sixty-eight species of birds and mammals in North America have been threatened with extinction since the sixteenth century, and 50 percent of those have gone extinct. In the fourteen cases in which people have attempted to recover an endangered species, however, only one species (7 percent) has gone extinct. The limited number of species that have recovered following protection under the ESA is not surprising when we consider the population dynamics of small populations. In fact, the record of stabilization, improvement, and recovery and the rarity of extinction following listing are quite surprising. Small populations, such as those listed under the ESA, are threatened by a number of stochastic processes that cannot be influenced by managers.[6] Demographic, genetic, and environmental stochasticity each contribute to extinction of small populations even after environmental conditions have improved and anthropogenic threats are removed. Therefore, during the initial phase of recovery, while populations are small, the probability of chance extinction exists even though the average rate of population growth is strongly positive. The black-footed ferret's (*Mustela nigripes*) recovery history provides a good example of a species increasing in abundance only to succumb to stochastic, uncontrollable variables.[7]

Extinctions have always occurred.[8] At least 90 percent of all species that have existed have disappeared.[9] Consequently, some argue, we cannot and should not legislate to stop natural processes. Most scientists agree, however, that today's extinction rates go far beyond "background" levels. Caughley and Gunn[10] calculated an average background extinction rate of 0.06 percent species lost every one thousand years. The mass extinction of the dinosaurs resulted from an extinction rate of one per one thousand years.[11] Extinction estimates for the last quarter of the twentieth century are over one hundred per day.[12] Nott et al.[13] and Hunter[14] concluded that based on conservative estimates, today's extinction rates are 10–1,000 times background levels and that future extinction rates could be even higher. Furthermore, the rate of extinctions is rapidly increasing,[15] and the extent and distribution of extinctions is unlike any previous major extinction period. Assuming human population stabilizes at 10–15 billion people in the next fifty to one hundred years and that ecosystems stabilize concomitantly, Wilson[16] believes we will lose 10–25 percent of our biota in an incredibly short period.

As demonstrated, many subjective variables interfere with our ability to evaluate the ESA's biological effectiveness. Bean[17] emphasized that the measure of progress in species conservation is "neither absolutely clear or quantifiable, nor is it likely identical for all species. These general observations are important to keep in mind if only to help resist the temptation to reach pre-mature judgments about the program as a whole based on success or setbacks involving individual species." Perhaps any apparent ineffectiveness lies not with the ESA but with the fact that the ESA is expected to accomplish too much on its own too late.[18] The National Research Council[19] also concluded that the "ESA cannot by itself prevent all species extinctions—even with modification." As we reviewed earlier, small populations are difficult to recover due to stochastic processes. Can we make the ESA more effective at lower costs? Effective biological conservation must begin prior to species decline.

By the time a species becomes eligible for listing, its habitat is often destroyed or badly degraded, the population is decimated, and its genetic diversity seriously eroded.[20] Additional delays in developing and implementing recovery plans under the ESA further imperil species. Recovery plans are often not developed for years, if at all.[21] The lack of biological information further hampers the listing and recovery plan process.[22] Lacking a national biological survey, knowledge on species' abundance and distribution is limited. More important, information on trends in species abundance is lacking. A thorough analysis of recovery plans and goals suggests that more than half of listed vertebrates would remain in serious risk of extinction even after meeting population targets in their recovery plans.[23] Delisting targets are often based on political expediency, not on biological or demographic evidence. These drawbacks, however, are not shortcomings of the ESA but of its implementation. Furthermore, target populations create an impression of certainty belied by the uncertainty of techniques used to estimate population levels. In addition, static goals can induce complacency once they are reached, a complacency incompatible with other factors involved, such as stochastic factors.[24]

Protection at an earlier level than that legislated by the ESA may be more effective for species conservation. Because habitat degradation and loss is a primary cause of extinction,[25] habitat preservation is often a primary concern of scientists and conservationists. The Ecological Society of America ad hoc committee[26] recommended that preservation of biological diversity be approached in a more proactive manner. They recommended identifying habitats and biological communities that are being seriously reduced in area or are being otherwise degraded and then establishing policies that prevent further losses of the habitats and restore degraded parts. They emphasized that such an approach could not replace a species-by-species approach, but that the number of species considered for listing should be greatly reduced. Identifying imperiled habitats in a proactive manner also makes more options available to managers. The Ecological Society of America committee advocated new complementary legislation for ecosystem-level protection that could help reverse the slide toward extinction by preventing habitat degradation. Such legislation would then allow the ESA to function as a safety net for those species whose survival cannot be guaranteed within protected ecosystems. While ecosystem approaches may sound appealing, their application will not be trouble free. Caughley and Gunn[27] argue that the vagueness of the term *ecosystems* will render it unworkable and that species must remain the cornerstone of conservation efforts.

Belovsky et al.,[28] however, stated that "although the preservation of suitable habitat is necessary, it may no longer be sufficient to ensure the recovery of small populations." They emphasized that the initial cause for reduced populations is a different problem from concerns for the persistence or recovery of precarious populations. Special demographic and genetic traits of small populations are integral factors of population viability analysis and recovery prospects. In their analysis of endangered species that survived versus endangered species that went extinct, 74 percent of those going extinct were restricted to small areas versus 35 percent of those that survived. Habitat approaches to conservation will need to involve larger areas than is customary today, and management will need to be action, not preservation, oriented.[29]

ECONOMIC IMPACT OF THE ESA

When initially enacting the 1973 ESA, Congress explicitly noted that economic criteria would not be included in either the listing or the designation of proposed critical habitat. In fact, the U.S. Supreme Court ruled in *Tennessee Valley Authority v. Hill* that " . . . it is clear from the Act's legislative history that Congress intended to halt and reverse the trend toward species extinction—whatever the cost." [30] Not until the 1978 amendments did economics enter explicitly into the ESA. First, under Section 4— Determination of endangered species and threatened species, the secretary of the interior may "take into consideration the economic impact, and any other relevant impact, of specifying any particular area as critical habitat" for a threatened or endangered species. The secretary can exclude an area from critical habitat designation if he or she determines that the benefits of exclusion outweigh the benefits to specifying the critical habitat, "unless failure to designate leads to extinction." Second, under Section 7—Interagency cooperation, a federal agency, the governor of a state, or a permit or license applicant may apply to the secretary for an exemption from the ESA. The secretary then submits a report to an ESA committee that discusses, among other things, the availability of reasonable and prudent alternatives to the agency's proposed action, and "the nature and extent of the benefits" of the action and proposed alternatives. [31]

Three executive orders [32] requiring the assessment of costs and benefits of different regulatory actions have forced decision makers to acknowledge the existence of the overall private and social costs and benefits of listing species, designating critical habitat, and implementing recovery plans for the species listed by the ESA. We now explore what we know and do not know about the basic costs and benefits of the ESA. One point to keep in mind is that a significant fraction of the ESA costs is often borne by property owners whose land is inhabited by endangered species, while the ESA benefits accrue to the entire nation, given the "public good" nature of the services provided by endangered species.

Costs of the ESA

The economic costs of the ESA to private property owners can be categorized into three broad areas: actual expenditures, opportunity costs of restricted land use, and opportunity costs of public expenditures on endangered species. The actual expenditures to the private property owners from the ESA are transaction costs arising from the time and money spent applying for permits and licenses, redesigning plans, and paying legal fees. As of now, no estimate of these transaction costs exists in the literature. As a comparison, Rich[33] estimated that the private legal expenditures incurred in battling the enforcement of the Comprehensive Environmental Response, Compensation, and Liability Act was over $8 billion just up to 1984, enough to clean an additional four hundred Superfund sites.

Opportunity costs are the more accurate measure of the economic impact of the ESA, since they measure the forgone opportunities of the property owner due to restrictions on the use of private property created by listings, designation of critical habitat, and recovery plans. If a listed species is found on private land such that a current or proposed action is no longer viable, the property owner suffers an opportunity cost. These opportunity costs include the reduced economic rents from restricted or altered development projects, agriculture production, timber harvesting, minerals extraction, or recreation activities; wages lost by displaced workers who remain unemployed or who are reemployed at lower wages; lower consumer surplus due to higher prices; and lower county property and severance tax revenue. For example, the Bonneville Power Administration estimated that its expenditure on salmon conservation was about $350 million in 1994 (1 percent of 1994 revenues), of which about $300 million represented the opportunity cost of lost power revenues.[34]

At present, there is no national estimate of the opportunity costs to private property owners due to the ESA. One study that does not estimate the national opportunity costs of the ESA but rather explores the association between the ESA and national economic growth is Meyer's.[35] Based on an econometric analysis of economic growth trends in all fifty states between 1975 and 1990, Meyer argues that the effect of the ESA has not been detrimental to economic development, since a negative relationship was not found between ESA listings and either construction employment or gross state product. For example, Alabama, with seventy listed species, had a booming economy, while Louisiana, with twenty-one listings, did poorly. If anything, Meyer suggests a positive relationship between growth and listings even when accounting for relative land areas, dependence on natural resource industries, size of the economy, and changes in the number of listings over time. But since Meyer's study does not measure the opportunity costs of the ESA as defined by the difference in actual economic growth with the ESA and potential economic growth without the ESA, these results need to be taken with caution. Without such an opportunity-cost estimate, we cannot conclude that the ESA has not had a significant economic impact on the national economy.

The existing economic literature that attempts to estimate the regional opportunity-cost impacts of the ESA does not separate out impacts on private property owners from those on operators of public lands. First, Rubin et al.[36] estimate the short-run and long-run opportunity costs of northern spotted owl protection to Washington and Oregon. Short-run costs include the value of timber forgone plus the additional costs of displaced workers, whose numbers range from 13,272 lost jobs by 1995 to over 28,000 by 2000. Long-run costs include only the value of the timber forgone, as these displaced workers will find other positions (assumed at an equivalent wage rate). In Washington and Oregon, the estimated short-run costs are $1.2 billion and long-run costs are $450 million.

Montgomery et al.[37] also estimate the opportunity costs of increasing the survival odds of the northern spotted owl. Creating a biological relationship to predict owl-survival odds based on habitat capacity, and employing the widely used Timber Assessment Market Model that projects prices and consumption and production trends in North American softwood, plywood, and stumpage markets, they compare how increased survival odds decrease economic welfare as measured by the present value of altered revenues, incomes, and consumer surplus (i.e., the difference between what a consumer is willing to pay and what he actually has to pay). According to their analysis, a recovery plan that increases the survival odds to 91 percent for about 1,600 to 2,400 owl pairs will decrease economic welfare by $33 billion (1990 dollars), with a disproportionate share of the losses borne by the regional producers of intermediate wood products, a relatively small segment of the population. If the recovery plan attempts to increase the survival odds to 95 percent, welfare losses increase to $46 billion.

Using an input-output modeling system, Brookshire et al.[38] perform economic analyses of critical habitat designation in the (1) Virgin River basin for the wound fin, Virgin River chub, and Virgin spinedace, and (2) Colorado River basin for the razorback sucker, humpback chub, Colorado squawfish, and bonytail. In the Virgin River study, they found that the present value of output changes in the Washington County (Utah) economy due to the designation of critical habitat for fish is about −$48 million, which represents 0.0016 percent of the present value of the baseline stream of output. Employment and earning effects are similar in magnitude. The effect in Clark County (Nevada) of critical habitat designation is of an even smaller magnitude, 0.00001 percent of the baseline economic activity. For the entire region, effects on the output, employment, earnings, and tax revenue are similar in magnitude: 0.0001 percent decline of the baseline activity.

Brookshire et al. found similar results for the Colorado River basin. Three conclusions emerge: First, the difference in total economic output with and without critical habitat designation is 0.0003 percent. Similar results hold for earnings income, tax revenues, and employment. Second, the impact of critical habitat designation is not evenly distributed across the states in the basin, as streamflow requirements may negatively impact recreation, electric power production, and future consumptive use in some states but enhance these activities in other states. Third, the national impacts of the designation are negligible.

Finally, public funds not spent on endangered species can be spent on something else, something viewed as potentially more valuable to the general public. Public expenditures for the ESA arise from conservation programs and the implementation of recovery plans for specific species. The Fish and Wildlife Service estimates that about $177 million was spent on endangered species conservation programs in 1991; what this amount covers, however, is unclear.[39] FWS spending on endangered and threatened species has increased three times faster than inflation since 1974, with much of the growth occurring in the 1970s.[40] The FWS's budget for recovery plans, including land acquisition, management, and research, was $10.4 million in 1991 and $39.7 million in 1995.[41] But the exact amount of money spent on recovery costs is more difficult to locate in the literature. For example, Clark et al.[42] present case studies of recovery plans for seven endangered species, including black-footed ferrets and Yellowstone grizzly bears, and aside from a few brief mentions of annual budgets and inadequate funding, there was not one estimate of the total actual monetary expenditures of these recovery plans. Overall, the U.S. Department of the Interior estimated that the potential direct costs from the recovery plans of all listed species amounted to about $4.6 billion.[43]

The General Accounting Office[44] recently compiled estimates of the predicted actual costs (i.e., direct outlays) and time needed to recover selected species, including the costs of implementing the most important recovery actions. The GAO reported on fifty-eight approved recovery plans, finding that thirty-four plans had a total-cost estimate for carrying out the recovery, twenty-three plans had cost estimates for the initial years of recovery, and one had a cost estimate for one part of a twelve-part plan. Of the thirty-four total-cost estimates, the amounts ranged from a 1994 cost of $145,000 for the White River spinedace (a fish) to a 1991 estimate of about $154 million for the green sea turtle and loggerhead turtle. The total estimated cost for the thirty-four species is approximately $700 million. For the twenty-three plans with initial three-year estimates, costs range from a 1990 estimate of $57,000 for the Florida scrub jay to a 1991 estimate of $49.1 million for the black-capped vireo (a bird). The three-year total cost for the twenty-three species is over $350 million. For the "high-priority" actions, the total estimated cost is about $223 million for three years.

Note that FWS and the National Marine Fisheries Service, worried that these numbers would be taken out of context, attached several caveats to these cost estimates. First, they pointed out that these estimates are for high-priority species and are therefore unrepresentative of the vast majority of species with recovery plans projected to be less expensive. Second, they argued that the cost estimates are just that . . . estimates, best guesses that are not subject to strict economic analysis. This begs the question of why economists are not included as part of the recovery planning team. Third, estimated costs differ considerably from actual costs due to revisions in recovery plans.

Of the money actually expended on endangered species recovery by federal and state agencies between 1989 and 1991 (1989 was the first year data were published), over 50 percent was spent on the top ten species: bald eagle ($31.3 m), northern spotted owl ($26.4 m), Florida scrub jay ($19.9 m), West Indian manatee ($17.3 m), red-cockaded woodpecker ($15.1 m), Florida panther ($13.6 m), grizzly bear ($12.6 m), least bell's vireo ($12.5 m), American peregrine falcon ($11.6 m), and whooping crane ($10.8 m).[45] In fact, over 95 percent of identifiable expenditures have been on vertebrates, causing Metrick and Weitzman[46] to suggest that visceral characteristics play a greater role than scientific characteristics in governmental spending decisions on individual species.

Benefits of the ESA

Environmental resources provided by endangered species on private property can supply a flow of direct and indirect private and social benefits to the property owner. The services provided by these endangered species and their corresponding levels of biological diversity are multifarious, ranging from basic life support to new genetic material for pharmaceutical purposes. These resources provide a nearly limitless set of valuable services; some private services are priced through the market based on their commercial or consumptive value, but many of their public services remain unpriced by the market. These public services are rarely bought and sold by the pound on the auction block and therefore never enter into private markets and remain unpriced by the public sector. For example, the market price of land does not generally account for the complete value of wildlife habitat services if the associated costs and benefits accrue to more than just the owner of the land. Wildlife does not stay within the confines of one owner's property. This inability to exclude others from enjoying benefits or suffering costs prevents the market price from sending the correct signal about the true value of the endangered species.

To some people, the private and social benefits of endangered species are so obvious that total benefits need not be measured. The essential ecological services of regulating climate, filtering water, maintaining soil fertility, pollinating crops, and other life-supporting functions are so valuable that the benefits of preservation will always exceed the benefits of development. This view is supported by Roughgarden: "In fact, we *should not* take costs into account when setting environmental (or other) objectives, but we should take costs into account when considering how to implement moral objectives as policy" (emphasis in original).[47] Essentially, the morality of environmental stewardship is not subject to benefit-cost analysis. If one accepts this view, then planners should attempt to establish a safe minimum standard, that is, the level of preservation that guarantees survival of the species in question.[48] The safe minimum standard essentially puts endangered species beyond the reach of economic tradeoffs, and the goal then becomes estimating the least costly solution to achieve this standard. The safe-minimum strategy becomes the practical alternative to optimal resource allocation.[49]

To others, however, the benefits of preservation may not outweigh the benefits of development. This view is exemplified by Epstein,[50] who argues:

Some people believe that it is important to develop nature to the full, to overcome poverty and to ensure prosperity; others believe that nature should be left in its original condition to the extent that that is possible, even if it means a cutback in overall standards of living. It is not within the power of either side to convert the doubters to the opposite position, and coercive systems of regulation are the worst possible way to achieve uniform social outcomes in the face of social disagreement. The interconnectedness of what goes on in one place and what goes on in another cannot be presumed on some dubious theory of necessary physical linkages for all events.

For these individuals, estimation of the private and social benefits of endangered species is paramount. They want more evidence that the benefits of preservation outweigh the benefits of development.

Private benefits to property owners include commercial use, consumptive use, and recreation. Two major commercial uses are the potential value in new pharmaceutical products from endangered species, and recreation. First, consider the value of genetic material for medicine. Genetic material from a species provides leads to help create better synthetic chemicals. Examples include the drug vincristine derived from the rare plant called the rosy periwinkle; taxol, a drug produced from the Pacific yew tree that is used in ovarian cancer treatment—a market estimated to reach $1 billion in 1996;[51] alkaloids from the Houston toad that may help reduce heart attacks; and the fatty acids from salmon useful for blood pressure and cholesterol control.[52]

Simpson et al.[53] provide one of the first systematic economic models to estimate the value of a marginal species for use in pharmaceutical research. They estimate the maximum value of a marginal species at about $9,400, given a model based on a series of independent statistical trials with equal probability of success, and using the parameters of 250,000 sampled species, ten expected new products arising from the genetics in these species, $300 million in costs of research and development, $450 million in revenue from the new products, and a 10 percent discount rate. They note that the value of a marginal species is very sensitive to the probability of success—an order-of-magnitude increase in the probability of a successful "hit" causes the value of a marginal species to decline to less than $0.0000005. Substitution opportunities are the key to understanding why an increased likelihood of a profitable species reduces the value of a marginal species. As one species substitutes for another in potential market success, the value of an expansive species exploration declines because it is likely that the firm will find a profitable species more quickly.

Another private benefit is the commercial and recreational harvesting of species. For example, commercial and recreational fishing for salmon in the Pacific Northwest helps support 60,000 jobs and over $1 billion in personal income in the regional economy.[54] Recreation benefits also exist in the form of ecotourism—ecotourists are willing to pay to view, or at least to have a high likelihood of viewing, rare species, as in the $200 million California whale-watching industry.

Estimating the social value of endangered species, however, presents a more challenging exercise due to (1) the problems of assigning economic value to goods that most people will never directly use, and (2) the controversial methods used to elicit these values. Economists have a distinct and well-defined definition of economic value based on the ideals of rationality and consumer sovereignty—the rational consumer is purposive and is best able to make the choices that affect his or her own welfare. But how can we attach an economic value to the mere existence of an environmental good that we may never use directly or even visit?

Following Krutilla,[55] economists have answered this question by proposing the concept of *total value*, which is the idea that consumers have both use and nonuse values for environmental resources. Use value is straightforward: the economic value of current commercial, consumptive, or recreational use. But estimating the level of a nonuse value is more problematic and controversial. *Option value* is the economic value of potential future use of a resource, while *existence value* is the value of its mere existence, with no plans to ever use it. As academicians debated the theoretical justification, the United States District of Columbia Court of Appeals ruled in 1989 that nonuse value constitutes a valid representation of economic value. In *Ohio v. U.S. Department of the Interior*,[56] the court stated that " . . . option and existence values may represent 'passive use' but they nonetheless reflect utility derived by humans from a resource and thus prima facie ought to be included in a damage assessment."

If we accept the idea that total value is a valid measure of the social benefits of endangered species, one tool to elicit these values is the controversial contingent valuation method. CVM directly elicits value by constructing a hypothetical market for a nonmarket good through the use of a survey. A hypothetical market attempts to create an opportunity for an individual to reveal his or her maximum willingness to pay or minimum willingness to accept compensation for a change in the level of the good. The survey is constructed so that features of actual markets and institutions are used to describe what the good is, how it will be changed, who will change it, how long the change will occur, and who will pay for the change. The major advantage of CVM is its flexibility to construct a market where no market currently exists. But flexibility is also the major weakness of CVM, as it allows ample opportunity for misperception. A researcher can specify a hypothetical good and elicit a value, but a respondent hypothetical value may be based on perceptions of the good that are quite different than expected by the researcher. Alternatively, indirect methods based on actual market data can also be used to estimate benefits of endangered species if some degree of complementarity or substitutability exists between the species and an actual market good.[57] Actual market data would include the costs of traveling to view an endangered species or the fraction of land or housing value that could be attributed to the nearby existence of a species, although until some incentive schemes are established to reward those private property owners who protect species, this value is likely to be negative. Most studies using market data have focused on wildlife, rain forests, and ecotourism outside the United States.[58]

Loomis and White[59] summarize the few CVM studies that have attempted to value an endangered species. They report evidence that the average individual's lump sum willingness to pay ranges from $12.99 to avoid the loss of the sea turtle (which one is not clear) to over $254 to increase the population of the bald eagle; the average individual's annual willingness to pay ranges from $6 to avoid the loss of the striped shiner to over $95 to avoid the loss of the northern spotted owl. Based on a 23 percent response rate to a CVM survey, Rubin et al.[60] estimated that the aggregate benefit of preserving the northern spotted owl was about $100 million for residents of Washington and Oregon and was about $1.5 billion for the total United States.[61]

But total value as measured by CVM has opponents who argue that total value is not really a measure of value of any particular environmental asset or endangered species. Instead it is a surrogate measure of general preferences toward the environment, a "warm glow" effect. Eliciting existence values with a contingent valuation survey provides the opportunity for a respondent to state his or her general preference toward the environment rather than for the specific species in question. This is often the first, if not only, occasion the person has been asked to reveal a public opinion on the environment, and as such, the value revealed may reflect the warm glow of contributing to save the general environment rather than the particular species at issue.

The exchange between Kahneman and Knetsch[62] and Smith[63] further illustrates the debate. Kahneman and Knetsch observed that the average willingness to pay to clean up one lake in Ontario was not significantly greater than the willingness to pay to clean up all the lakes in the province. They cite this as evidence that individuals are not responding to the good, but rather to the idea of contributing to environmental preservation in general, or the warm glow. Smith questioned this view, arguing that incremental willingness to pay should decline with the amount of the good already available, and as such the evidence is consistent with economic theory. But other controversial reports, such as that of Desvousges et al.,[64] support the warm-glow argument, finding evidence that the average willingness to pay to prevent 2,000 birds from dying in oil-filled ponds was not significantly different than the value to prevent 20,000 or 200,000 birds from dying. While accepting the argument that willingness to pay for additional protection probably does decline, Arrow et al.[65] note that the drop to zero "is hard to explain as the expression of a consistent, rational set of choices." In another example, Crocker and Shogren[66] find evidence of surrogate bidding for atmospheric visibility in Oregon, observing no significant difference in values for improved visibility in one specific mountain location as compared to the value for state-wide improvements. After examining a vast number of CVM studies, Arrow et al.[67] note that the bimodal distribution of value estimates—zero or a positive value around $30 to $50—suggests that these values may serve a function similar to charitable contributions. Not only does the respondent want to support a worthy cause, but he or she also receives a warm glow from donating to the cause.

Finally, there are several other issues involved with estimating the social value of endangered species. First, a piecemeal species-by-species approach will most likely overestimate economic value because it does not address potential substitution and adaptation possibilities. Going back to Loomis and White,[68] if we were to sum the average stated values of the eighteen species and to multiply this grand willingness to pay ($953) by the number of households in the United States (about 96 million), we would get a total benefit estimate of $91 billion in 1993 dollars, over 1 percent of the 1995 U.S. Gross National Product of over $7 trillion. Even if we just focus on the five studies in which people were asked to state a one-time lump-sum payment for either bald eagles, humpback whales, monk seals, gray wolves, or arctic grayling/cutthroat trout, the national benefit estimate is $44 billion (1993 dollars). The summed values of five unique studies over each species will most likely exceed the value of one study valuing these five endangered species together. Hoehn and Loomis[69] find that independent aggregation of the benefits of only two programs overstates their total benefits by 27 percent; the overstatement with three programs is 54 percent. We need to better understand the relationship between the values for species and their substitution/adaptation possibilities before any national estimate of nonuse values will be useful in the ESA debate.

Second, even if we get beyond warm glows and elicit meaningful values for endangered species, we must still acknowledge that many individuals are unfamiliar with most of the services and functions that ecosystems and biodiversity provide. As an example, a survey of Scottish citizens revealed that over 70 percent of the respondents were completely unfamiliar with the meaning of biodiversity.[70] Such levels of unfamiliarity are of concern if consumer sovereignty is to command respect in resource policy questions. Third, benefit estimation should account for the fact that the resource-allocation decisions each of us makes today generate costs and benefits that can accrue far into the future. Although scientists and policymakers have questioned the use of individuals' preferences toward the present to construct social discount rates, they nevertheless acknowledge their importance. If we do not understand how individuals actually discount the future consequences of their choices, endangered species policy that ignores individuals' preferences toward the present guarantees unintended results.[71]

CONCLUSIONS

At a national level, the biological effectiveness and economic impacts of the ESA are unknown at this date. No one has even attempted a back-of-the-envelope guess, however crude. On the biological side, this refusal to hypothesize is driven by the lack of an objective measure of biological effectiveness and by insufficient time to judge the overall success of the different species recovery plans. On the economic side, our conjectures are restrained by the lack of any estimates of the national costs and benefits of protecting all of the nearly 1,125 listed species; we have not computed the transaction costs, opportunity costs of restricted property rights, opportunity costs of public funds used in species recovery, nor the subsequent economic benefits from the current listings decisions, critical habitat designations, or recovery plans. Obvious research priorities are to estimate both the national economic costs and benefits of the ESA by integrating our economic tools with a viable set of ecological indicators.[72]

A final note: We have examined the economic impact of the ESA through the narrow lens of standard cost-benefit analysis. It is worth remembering, however, that this standard analysis is embedded in a more general economic framework that considers the consequences of selecting alternative institutions and property-right configurations that promote one end over another. As we begin to address the broader trade-offs of secure property rights and protection of endangered species, we will need to move beyond measuring the consequences of the status quo to capturing the trade-offs between two polar views of incommensurability. One person's inalienable right to protection of endangered species will need to be balanced against another's inalienable right of self-determination. This will become the critical question in the ESA reauthorization debate. Effectively addressing this question will require the policymakers to further develop and support institutions that promote cooperative solutions based on both biology and economics.

NOTES

The comments of Tom Crocker and Steve Gloss have been helpful. Jeff Petry performed valuable research assistance.

1   P. Ehrlich and A. Ehrlich, The Value of Biodiversity, *Ambio* 21(1992):219–226.
2   G. Caughley and A. Gunn, *Conservation Biology in Theory and Practice* (London: Blackwell Science, 1996).
3   Fish and Wildlife Service, *Report to Congress: Endangered and Threatened Species Recovery Program* (Washington, D.C.: U.S. Government Printing Office, 1994).
4   National Research Council, *Science and the Endangered Species Act* (Washington, D.C.: National Academy Press, 1995).
5   G. E. Belovsky, J. A. Bissonette, R. D. Dueser, T. Edwards Jr., C. M. Lueke, M. E. Ritchie, J. B. Slade, and F. H. Wagner, Management of Small Populations: Concepts Affecting the Recovery of Endangered Species, *Wildlife Society Bulletin* 22(1994):307–316.
6   See reviews by Belovsky et al., Management of Small Populations, 307–316. Caughley and Gunn, *Conservation Biology in Theory and Practice.*
7   Caughley and Gunn, *Conservation Biology in Theory and Practice.*
8   M. J. Benton, Diversification and Extinction in the History of Life, *Science* 268(1995):52–58.
9   N. Meyers, *The Sinking Ark: A New Look at the Problem of Disappearing Species* (New York: Pergamon Press, 1979).
10 Caughley and Gunn, *Conservation Biology in Theory and Practice.*
11 Meyers, *The Sinking Ark.*
12 Ibid.

· 13   M. Nott, E. Rogers, and S. Pimm, Modern Extinctions in the Kilo-Death Range, *Current Biology* 5(1995):14–17.

14   M. L. Hunter Jr., *Fundamentals of Conservation Biology* (Cambridge, Mass.: Blackwell Science, 1996).

15   G. Nilsson, *The Endangered Species Handbook* (Washington, D.C.: The Animal Welfare Institute, 1983).

16   E. O. Wilson, *The Diversity of Life* (Cambridge, Mass.: Belknap Press of Harvard University Press, 1992).

17   M. J. Bean, The Endangered Species Program, *Audubon Wildlife Report 1986,* ed. R. L. DiSilvestro (New York: National Audubon Society, 1986), pp. 347–371.

18   T. H. Tear, J. M. Scott, P. H. Hayward, and B. Griffith, Status and Prospects for Success of the Endangered Species Act: A Look at Recovery Plans, *Science* 262(1993):976–977.

   NRC, *Science and the Endangered Species Act.*

   R. Carroll, C. Augspurger, A. Dobson, J. Franklin, G. Orians, W. Reid, R. Tracy, D. Wilcove, and J. Wilson, Strengthening the Use of Science in Achieving the Goals of the Endangered Species Act: An Assessment by the Ecological Society of America, *Ecological Applications* 6(1996):1–11.

   Belovsky et al., Management of Small Populations.

19   NRC, *Science and the Endangered Species Act.*

20   Carroll et al., Strengthening the Use of Science in Achieving the Goals of the Endangered Species Act.

   Bean, The Endangered Species Program.

   Belovsky et al., Management of Small Populations.

21   Carroll et al., Strengthening the Use of Science in Achieving the Goals of the Endangered Species Act.

22   Tear et al., Status and Prospects for Success of the Endangered Species Act.

   T. H. Tear, J. M. Scott, P. H. Hayward, and B. Griffith, Recovery Plans and the Endangered Species Act: Are Criticisms Supported by Data? *Conservation Biology* 9(1995):182–195.

23   Tear et al., Status and Prospects for Success of the Endangered Species Act.

24   Caughley and Gunn, *Conservation Biology in Theory and Practice.*

25   J. Terborgh and B. Winter, Some Causes of Extinction, *Conservation Biology: An Evolutionary-Ecological Perspective,* ed. M. E. Soule and B. A. Wilcox (Sunderland, Mass.: Sinauer, 1980), pp. 119–133.

   Caughley and Gunn, *Conservation Biology in Theory and Practice.*

26   Carroll et al., Strengthening the Use of Science in Achieving the Goals of the Endangered Species Act.

27   Caughley and Gunn, *Conservation Biology in Theory and Practice.*

28   Belovsky et al., Management of Small Populations.

29   Ibid.

30   See J. Souder, Chasing Armadillos Down Yellow Lines: Economics in the Endangered Species Act, *Natural Resources Journal* 33(1993):1095–1139.

31   See P. Baldwin, *Consideration of Economic Factors under the Endangered Species Act* (Washington, D.C.: Congressional Research Service, Library of Congress, 1989).

32   Exec. Order No. 11,821, 3 C.F.R. 203 (1974), reprinted in 2 U.S.C. § 1904

(repealed); Exec. Order No. 12,291, 3 C.F.R. 127 (1981), reprinted in 5 U.S.C. § 601 (repealed); Exec. Order No. 12,630, 3 C.F.R. 554 (1988), reprinted in 5 U.S.C. § 601 (1994).

33 B. Rich, Environmental Litigation and the Insurance Dilemma, *Risk Management* 32(1985):34–41.

34 NRC, *Science and the Endangered Species Act.*

35 S. Meyer, Endangered Species Listings and State Economic Performance, working paper (Cambridge, Mass.: Massachusetts Institute of Technology, 1995).

36 J. Rubin, G. Helfand, and J. Loomis, A Benefit-Cost Analysis of the Northern Spotted Owl, *Journal of Forestry* 89(1991):25–30.

37 C. Montgomery, G. Brown Jr., and M. Darius, The Marginal Cost of Species Preservation: The Northern Spotted Owl, *Journal of Environmental Economics and Management* 26(1994):111–128.

38 D. Brookshire, M. McKee, and C. Schmidt, Draft Economic Analyses of Critical Habitat Designation in the Virgin River Basin for the Woundfin, Virgin River Chub, and Virgin Spinedace, Report to the U.S. Fish and Wildlife Service, 1995.
    D. Brookshire, M. McKee, and G. Watts, An Economic Analysis of Critical Habitat Designation in the Colorado River Basin for the Razorback Sucker, Humpback Chub, Colorado Squawfish, and Bonytail, Final Report to the U.S. Fish and Wildlife Service, 1994.

39 NRC, *Science and the Endangered Species Act.*

40 F. Campbell, The Appropriations History, in *Balancing on the Brink of Extinction: The Endangered Species Act and Lessons for the Future,* ed. K. Kohm (Washington, D.C.: Island Press, 1991), pp. 134–146.

41 NRC, *Science and the Endangered Species Act.*

42 T. Clark, R. Reading, and A. Clarke, eds., *Endangered Species Recovery: Finding the Lessons, Improving the Process* (Washington, D.C.: Island Press, 1994).

43 FWS, *Report to Congress: Endangered and Threatened Species Recovery Program* (Washington, D.C.: U.S. Government Printing Office, 1990).

44 General Accounting Office, Correspondence to Representative Don Young on Estimated Recovery Costs of Endangered Species, B-270461, Washington, D.C., 1995.

45 See A. Metrick and M. Weitzman, Patterns of Behavior in Endangered Species Preservation, *Land Economics* 72(1996):1–16.

46 Ibid.

47 See p. 153 in J. Roughgarden, Can Economics Protect Biodiversity? in *The Economics and Ecology of Biodiversity Decline,* ed. T. Swanson (Cambridge: Cambridge University Press, 1995), pp. 149–154.

48 S. Ciriacy-Wantrup, *Resource Conservation: Economics and Policies* (Berkeley: University of California, 1952).

49 R. Bishop, Economic Efficiency, Sustainability, and Biodiversity, *Ambio* 22(1993):69–73.

50 See R. Epstein, *Simple Rules for a Complex World* (Cambridge, Mass.: Harvard University Press, 1995), p. 278.

51 R. Norton, Owls, Trees, and Ovarian Cancer, *Fortune* 2, no. 5(1995):49.

52 W. R. Irvin, Statement to United States Senate Committee on Environmental

and Public Works, Subcommittee on Drinking Water, Fisheries, and Wildlife, 13 July 1995.

53   R. Simpson, R. Sedjo, and J. Reid, Valuing Biodiversity for Use in Pharmaceutical Research, *Journal of Political Economy* 104(1996):163–185.

54   Irvin, Statement to United States Senate Committee on Environmental and Public Works, Subcommittee on Drinking Water, Fisheries, and Wildlife.

55   J. Krutilla, Conservation Reconsidered, *American Economic Review* 57(1967): 787–796.

56   880 F.2d 432, 464 (D.C. Cir. 1989).

57   See J. Braden and C. Kolstad, eds., *Measuring the Demand for Environmental Quality* (Amsterdam: North-Holland, 1991); and G. Peterson, C. Swanson, D. McCollum, and M. Thomas, eds., *Valuing Wildlife Resources in Alaska* (Boulder: Westview Press, 1992).

58   See, for example, M. Munasinghe, Biodiversity Protection Policy: Environmental Valuation and Distributional Issues, *Ambio* 21(1992):227–236.

59   J. Loomis and D. White, Economic Benefits of Rare and Endangered Species: Summary and Meta Analysis, photocopy (Fort Collins: Colorado State University, 1996).

60   Rubin, Helfand, and Loomis, A Benefit-Cost Analysis of the Northern Spotted Owl.

61   Also see D. Hagen, J. Vincent, and P. Welle, Benefits of Preserving Old-Growth Forests and the Spotted Owl, *Contemporary Policy Issues* 10(1992):13–25.

62   D. Kahneman and J. Knetsch, Valuing Public Goods: The Purchase of Moral Satisfaction, *Journal of Environmental Economics and Management* 22(1991):57–70.

63   V. K. Smith, Arbitrary Values, Good Causes, and Premature Verdicts, *Journal of Environmental Economics and Management* 22(1992):71–89.

64   W. Desvousges, F. R. Johnson, R. Dunford, K. Boyle, S. Hudson, and K. Wilson, *Measuring Natural Resource Damages with Contingent Valuation: Tests of Validity and Reliability* (Research Triangle, N.C.: Research Triangle Institute, 1992).

65   See K. Arrow, R. Solow, P. Portney, E. Leamer, R. Radner, and H. Schuman, Report of the NOAA Panel on Contingent Valuation, photocopy (Washington, D.C.: Resources for the Future, 1993), p. 11.

66   T. Crocker and J. Shogren, Ex Ante Valuation of Atmospheric Visibility, *Applied Economics* 23(1991):143–151.

67   K. Arrow, R. Solow, P. Portney, E. Leamer, R. Radner, and H. Schuman, Report of the NOAA Panel on Contingent Valuation, photocopy (Washington, D.C.: Resources for the Future, 1993).

68   Loomis and White, Economic Benefits of Rare and Endangered Species: Summary and Meta Analysis.

69   J. Hoehn and J. Loomis, Substitution Effects in the Valuation of Multiple Environmental Programs, *Journal of Environmental Economics and Management* 25(1993):56–75.

70   N. Hanley and C. Spash, The Value of Biodiversity in British Forests, Report to the Scottish Forestry Commission, University of Sterling, Scotland, 1993.

71   See, for example, T. Crocker and J. Shogren, Dynamic Inconsistency in Valuing Environmental Goods, *Ecological Economics* 7(1993):239–254.

N. Hanley, C. Spash, and L. Walker, Problems in Valuing the Benefits of Biodiversity Protection, *Environmental and Resource Economics* 5(1995):249–272.

72 J. W. Milon and J. Shogren, eds., *Integrating Economic and Ecological Indicators* (Westport, Conn.: Praeger Publishers, 1995).

❧ 5 ❧

The Intent and Implementation of the Endangered Species Act: A Matter of Scale

Jeffrey A. Lockwood

Levin[1] noted that "[scale is] the fundamental conceptual problem in ecology, if not in all of science." Often, what we believe to be opposing theories are a matter of equally valid concepts being advanced at different scales.[2] As such, when intelligent people's perceptions are in conflict, the tension may be a function of mismatched scales, rather than diametrically opposed philosophies. The debate that has arisen in the context of the application of the Endangered Species Act on private property may be such a conflict. It has been said that the ESA pits "the nation's fierce obsession with self-determination and private property versus its love of the wilderness and compassion for wildlife."[3]

The goal of this chapter is to take a scale-based perspective in examining the fundamental principles of the ESA and private property rights. The hazard in my using this approach is that, not being a social scientist, I may not fully appreciate the context of this conflict. The advantage is being able to bring an ecologist's perspective to an arena that has been dominated by development and commodity interests of the "wise-use" movement and various environmental organizations and animal rights groups that make up the Endangered Species Coalition.[4]

THE TEMPORAL SCALE

Conflicts of Intent

While opponents of the ESA point out that extinction is the ultimate fate of all species,[5] this truism fails to recognize that the current extinction rate is at least 1,000 times the normal rate of species loss.[6] Although the public may believe that our major environmental problems are solved,[7] the loss of species is unabated at a global level, with a loss of some twenty thousand species per year.[8] Due to the ESA, we have made demonstrable progress toward arresting this trend in the United States. Whereas over five hundred species are known to have been lost from the United States in the two hundred years prior to the act, only seven extinctions have been documented in this country in the twenty-one years since its passage.[9]

Even decade-long perspectives may be alien to those private property owners who purchase property as a short-term investment, without the intent to live on, let alone steward, the land.[10] Land speculation will be increasingly lucrative as our population continues to grow. Where lands are owned with the intent of sustaining their ecological functions (e.g., producing forage, crops, or timber) within a multigenerational family network, conflicts with the ESA will not disappear, but the time frame for constructive dialogue will not be defined by a race to convert the land to immediate anthropocentric use.

Conflicts of Implementation

Kubasek and Browne[11] noted that "[f]or many, the major problems arising from the Act stem not so much from any inherent flaws in the structure of the legislation, but rather from problems of enforcement and funding." This is a common notion, and it suggests that we can resolve species-property conflicts by creatively implementing the act. Even the process that permits harm to endangered species (i.e., habitat conservation plan) may often be viewed as a serious impediment to the property owner, who must act quickly to exploit opportunities to "develop" the land.[12] Although ESA procedures are extremely fast in terms of ecological time, the implementation of the act is viewed as cumbersome in economic timescales.

The timescale of the ESA is based on ecological processes, which are fundamentally slower than the rates of development and extractive projects on private property. The intent of the act is intergenerational, while the profits to be made on development of private property are often immediate. This is not to say that the ESA is disconnected from economic concerns. As noted by Watkins,[13] "The truth is that our economy depends on the sustained health of the environment. What is economic in the long run is what conserves endangered species"—a realization that is substantiated by the loss of forty thousand coastal fishery jobs with the decline of salmon, and the struggles of fruit growers in Guam who are overwhelmed by fruit flies that had been kept in check by a now endangered bat.[14]

The rate of species' recovery is a complex function of biological attributes,[15] and no legislation can change ecological timescales. Many endangered species have lost more than 90 percent of their habitat to anthropogenic factors in the last two hundred years,[16] and the ESA could not reasonably have led to the recovery of many of these species in just two decades.[17] This temporal difficulty has led to the suggestion that rather than reacting at the brink of extinction, we should take proactive measures to prevent such crises.[18] However, this dichotomy of tactics may be misleading; the "nick of time" context of the ESA is proactive to the extent that endangered species are warnings that entire communities and ecosystems are at risk.

The ESA has been criticized by conservation biologists for not having a sufficiently long temporal perspective. Shaffer[19] suggested that a population should be considered as viable if it has a 99 percent chance of surviving for one thousand years in the face of stochastic factors. But actions mandated by Sections 7 or 10 of the ESA are functionally limited to the applicant's project time frame, which may be unrelated to even short-term population trends.[20] The FWS was criticized for short-sightedness in defending their decision to delist the brown pelican based on the contention that mining impacts were unlikely in the *near* future.[21] In a similar fashion, offshore oil leases were permitted because the admitted harm to protected whales was not "sufficiently imminent or certain."[22]

THE SPATIAL SCALE

Conflicts of Intent

In global terms, tropical countries are experiencing the majority of extinctions by virtue of their biological richness and economic struggle.[23]

Given that the vast majority of our food, fiber, and medicines are derived from organisms that originated outside of our borders, the explicit recognition of international cooperation and conventions within the ESA is a matter of enlightened self-interest.[24] Although the ESA provides limited means of addressing international losses of biodiversity, the act was never intended to halt extinctions on a global scale, contrary to the implications of Kubasek and Browne.[25] The 1,125 endangered species in the United States are almost certainly just the tip of the "extinction iceberg" if we consider our nescience about insects, the most speciose group of organisms. Insects comprise over half of the known species,[26] but account for only 3 percent of the identified endangered species.[27]

The spatial scale of the ESA was intended to be predominantly national, comprehensively protecting species across ownership boundaries in an extraordinary attempt at national self-restraint.[28] However, because species on the verge of extinction are often limited to small tracts of land, the ESA (Sections 7 and 10) limits concern to the applicant's property boundary, a scale that may be unrelated to biogeographic constraints.[29] This presents a serious difficulty between the apparent intent of the act and the ecology of endangered species. In light of the large-scale importance of metapopulations with respect to buffering impacts, even species that appear to be locally stable may not be adequately protected.[30]

The FWS and National Marine Fisheries Service have maintained nearly 40 percent of listed species in stable or improving condition.[31] This success has been possible because the ESA is not limited to the myopic preservation of species (claims to the contrary notwithstanding[32]). Rather, the act is implemented at spatial scales that reflect the ecology of the species.[33]

Conflicts of Implementation

Although individual properties are often small, two-thirds of the United States is privately owned. Over one-third of all endangered species are found exclusively on private property, and about three-quarters of listed species rely on habitat found on these lands.[34] Therefore, it is surprising that the conflicts between the ESA and property owners are rare.[35] Only 0.005 percent of some 100,000 consultations have yielded jeopardy opinions that halted the federal actions.[36] From 1983 to 1994 there were four cases in which injunctions stopped or delayed activity on nonfederal lands as posing a threat to endangered species that were under FWS protection.[37] Although some factions have framed the debate as a trade-off between species and jobs,[38] most of the accounts used to create this win-lose scenario are demonstrably false.[39]

The implementation of the act typically begins with a localized remnant of a species, and the presumption seems to be that as the species recovers, its range will expand until the spatial scale assures survival. Thus, the spatial scale of the ESA may be very large, including many private property owners. Indeed, the Department of the Interior defends small land exemptions by arguing that most species will not survive on small tracts of land.[40] However, while temperate-zone species show less endemism than tropical life-forms, there is no guarantee that a fully recovered species will not exist entirely on the property owned by a single individual.

The spatial elements of the ESA and private property give rise to the conflict of scale, wherein individual property owners perceive their endeavors to be of nominal impact, but the nation's biological wealth depends on the aggregated actions of individual owners.[41] The interests of the nation are profoundly interwoven with the actions of individuals. As our population expanded into the last frontiers, the capacity of a property owner to act as an autonomous agent isolated from the public good was lost. This spatial reality leads us to a consideration of the element of complexity or connectedness, a vital parameter in ecological systems.

THE CONNECTEDNESS SCALE

Conflicts of Intent

Although the ESA explicitly includes ecosystems only in the preamble to the act, some analysts have argued that protecting species was only intended as a means to the ends of preserving biodiversity and ecosystem well-being.[42] Judicial interpretation and regulatory obligation in this regard were slow in coming,[43] but there has been acknowledgment of the role of ecosystems in the protection of biological diversity.[44] The 1978 Report of the House Committee on Merchant Marine and Fisheries stated that "the ultimate goal of the Act is the conservation of the ecosystem on which all species, whether endangered or not, depend for survival," and this notion has been formalized through a FWS and NMFS joint policy statement.[45] Recently, some conservation biologists have criticized the act for not focusing on the "larger picture" of ecosystems,[46] but given our relatively poor understanding of ecosystem processes, the roles of various species, and even what constitutes an "ecosystem,"[47] the protection of indicator and umbrella species[48] may provide the optimal balance between preserving that which we can define and that which ultimately sustains an ecosystem.

The connections between ourselves and other species are complex but generally fall into three categories: ecological services, marketable goods, and cultural context. As noted by Mann and Plummer,[49] "the web of species around us helps generate soil, regulate fresh water supplies, dispose of waste, and maintain the quality of the atmosphere. Pillaging nature to the point where it cannot perform these functions is dangerously foolish." Our direct dependence on biodiversity via the utilitarian value of food and medicine is incontrovertible.[50] Perhaps the least resolved but most compelling arguments are ethical and spiritual.[51] The intent of the ESA appears to recognize the first two connections, ecological services and marketable goods. In a succinct integration of these notions into a single framework, the National Wildlife Federation argues that protecting species is part of our civic responsibility.[52]

Conflicts of Implementation

Species, endangered or not, represent a form of common property, or public trust, that connects their "owners" with complex obligations that may conflict with the private property upon which these species are found. Great bodies of law in this area revolve around an ethic of moderation, proportionality, prudence, and responsibility to others who are entitled to share in a common resource.[53] In ecological terms, the implementation of the ESA appears to be reductionistic, with only an implicit recognition that biodiversity cannot be understood or managed as parts. However, even though protecting species does not assure the preservation of the affected ecosystems,[54] given the interconnections among components, preserving the "weak link" in the chain may be an effective means of sustaining otherwise intractably complex systems.

Beattie[55] has argued that endangered species are the symptoms of one of the most difficult and critical environmental problems that humans have ever faced, a position echoed by dozens of scientists. While the cause and extent of global warming, ozone holes, and carcinogenic contaminants provide rich fodder for scientific debate, there appears to be no serious dissension regarding the reality and impacts of the biodiversity crisis. In the words of Wilson,[56] "If the message of the ESA is that the miners' canaries are about to die and that people might want to change the way they do their mining, the bio-phobic response is: kill the canaries. The best scientific evidence available suggests that this is a risky answer."

Thus, to the extent that we are dependent on a biologically rich world, the implementation of the ESA would not appear to be in conflict with human interests. However, this presumes that connections between our human and ecosystem well-being, vis-à-vis species, are independent of time and space. In actuality, interdependencies increase with our spatio-temporal perspective. For example, my immediate happiness is unlikely to diminish with yesterday's extinction, but the condition of my children may become intimately connected to this loss in ways we cannot measure. While discounting the future may be a defensible strategy when applied in an economic context, it is not at all clear that we can discount moral value in this manner.

In this light, the implementation of the ESA is not the problem. That is, endangered species are warning flags, and it is our awareness of environmental degradation, not its occurrence, that is evoked by the ESA. To build on the argument of Beattie,[57] we can choose to rescind the ESA but we cannot repeal the laws of nature or deny the loss of species—there are essential limits to anthropogenic alterations.

A SUMMARY OF SCALE-BASED CONFLICTS

Figures 5.1 to 5.4 portray an oversimplified but informative synthesis of the perceptual scales that may be applied in the ESA conflict. The stereotypical characterizations are not intended to fully portray all perspectives—the concerns of individuals are often complex, overlapping, and inconsistent. However, the graphic models illustrate how conflicts might arise as a consequence of nonoverlapping scales of concern. The "classic" ESA perspective, at the time of listing, focuses on the long-term, small-scale interests of a single species (Figure 5.1). As a species recovers and the ESA is used in more "progressive" or holistic terms of habitat protection across the species' range, the spatial and complexity scales increase accordingly (Figure 5.2). Interestingly, the archetypal landowner perspective (e.g., a cabin in the mountains or a cottage by a lake; Figure 5.3) includes a somewhat broader perception of complexity but a shorter temporal scale than the classic ESA perspective. The formulaic private producer perspective (e.g., monocultural farming; Figure 5.4) is one of short-term profitability based on few species over a relatively restricted spatial area, which is virtually the reciprocal of the holistic perspective of the ESA. This analysis suggests that some consideration of the perceptions of selected classes of stakeholders may provide valuable insight with respect to conflicts arising from the ESA. The unique perspectives of at least three such groups (property owners, society, and biocentrists) can be brought to bear on the issues related to the ESA and private property. Although rational positions can be derived from the scale of each observer, their essential focus changes with scale.

From the perspective of the private property owner, the protection of an endangered species can involve the potential of a Fifth Amendment taking (e.g., the taking of the right to convert a habitat into a golf course). From this perspective, it makes sense to pit the species' commodity value against that of the proposed action,[58] However, including economic parameters in the listing process [59] is ultimately nonsensical. The endangered status of species is not a function of whether it interferes with profits. Recent attempts by Congress to avoid discovering the condition of species by eliminating the National Biological Survey or prohibiting it from using volunteers are similarly irrational.[60] What makes sense is the existing opportunity to adapt the implementation of the ESA to avoid financially devastating impacts to private owners. Critical habitat can be excluded on social and economic grounds unless it would cause extinction.[61]

The private property owner must bear the burden of protecting a species for the benefit of society but receives no direct compensation for this service. Individualizing costs while collectivizing the benefits is the basis for the "tragedy of the commons," which may lead to the destruction of the common resource.[62] Given that the uncertain anthropocentric benefits of protecting any particular species are spatiotemporally diffuse, it is not surprising that a means for compensating private property owners has yet to be developed. Such a system must take into account a complex assortment of issues, not the least of which is whether payment should be considered for *any* diminishment of economic value or whether some losses are a reasonable consequence of living in a human and biological community.[63]

The demands for compensation by a private property owner who views compliance with the ESA as a Fifth Amendment constitutional "taking" of prospective profits by hindering activities[64] would seem to be reasonable from the individual's perspective. However, as the perspective

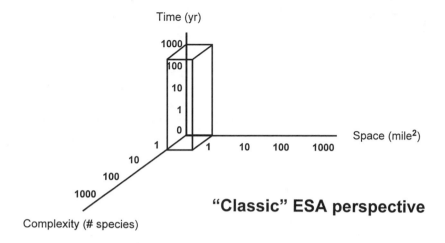

Figure 5.1. Stereotypical portrayal of the "classic" perspective of the ESA, in which a small remnant population of a single species is protected.

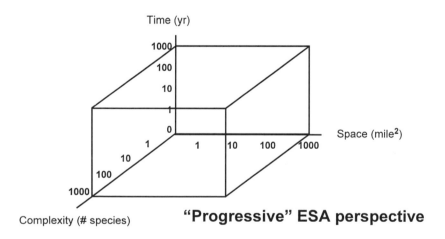

Figure 5.2. Stereotypical portrayal of the "progressive" perspective of the ESA, in which a recovering species is managed across its full range and in context of the entire biotic community.

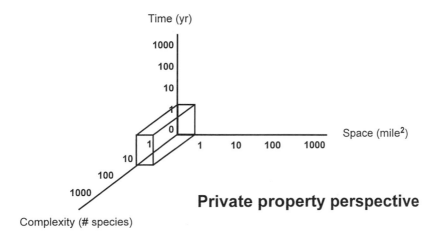

Figure 5.3. Stereotypical portrayal of the private property perspective of the land, in which an owner occupies property for noncommercial uses.

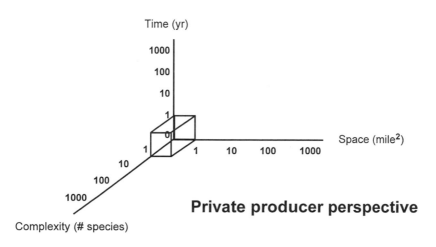

Figure 5.4. Stereotypical portrayal of the private producer perspective of the land, in which an owner produces a commodity on the property.

shifts to a social scale, this notion may collapse. Such individual claims would seem to be more than offset by the tens of billions of dollars provided by federal subsidies to private property owners. Direct support for development of private property (e.g., coastal housing developments, ski resorts, etc.) is considerable, but this subsidy is relatively modest compared with the massive tax credits to private property owners, which amounted to $74.4 billion in 1994.[65]

From a social perspective, the actions of the private property owner leading to an extinction may be perceived as a permanent taking of common property (i.e., the notion of the ESA Section 9 taking). From a national perspective, the act adopts a broad anthropocentric position in asserting that "[endangered] species are of aesthetic, ecological, educational, historical, recreational, and scientific value to the Nation and its people."[66] As we shall see, however, the ESA appears to capture much more than just instrumental value. Ultimately, the social perspective is utilitarian—we attempt to garner the greatest good for the greatest number. Our social and historical biases orient our utilitarianism to monetary units, which provide a uniform, if not entirely satisfactory, means of measuring value. While the economic analysis of the ESA from a public perspective is surely one of the most complex analytical tasks of our day, even basic budgetary issues are fraught with confusion.[67] Often, the necessary context is lacking, with the most dramatic economic impacts of the ESA paling in comparison to the downsizing of corporate America; the spotted owl may cost 9,000 jobs by 2010—IBM cut 36,000 jobs in 1994.[68] Notions that the act "demands a significant share of a federal budget"[69] are unfounded. Over the last two decades, on an annual basis the FWS and NMFS have never spent more on maintaining our biological infrastructure through the ESA than the cost of building 2–4 miles of federal interstate highway in the name of maintaining our transportation infrastructure.[70]

Our government has allocated about 2 percent of the funds needed to conduct recovery plans for all listed species.[71] The distribution of these limited funds is extremely skewed to the charismatic species; 270 plants and 89 invertebrates received just 5 percent of total funding.[72] One might argue that these allocations accurately reflect public concern, except that the federal funding for all endangered species is just 2.5 percent of the value our society places on a single endangered species, the whooping crane.[73] Based on this economic analysis, the most expensive recovery plan, which involves the green and loggerhead sea turtles, has a cost that is just 10 percent of our society's perceived value of the whooping crane, the only species for which such information is available.

From a biocentric perspective, many philosophers, including the pre-eminent conservation biologist Aldo Leopold, discount any attempts to justify species on economic grounds by arguing that "[t]o ask what a species is good for is the height of ignorance."[74] Although stories of the Pacific yew (a "trash" tree of the Pacific Northwest from which taxol, a potent treatment for breast and ovarian cancers, was derived) suggest the an-thropocentric value of some species, Mann and Plummer[75] note that no market will save the Oregon silverspot butterfly—it does not cure cancer, it isn't nutritious, and nobody will pay to see it. Although the ESA seems to fall short of explicitly acknowledging the intrinsic value of species, one might conclude that an implicit recognition of moral and spiritual values arises from the denial of purely instrumental values.[76] According to the Supreme Court, the act was "a conscious decision by Congress to give endangered species priority over 'primary missions' of federal agencies [and prevent extinction] whatever the cost."[77] As such, it has been argued that the ESA threatens the moral authority of hu-mans by questioning our independence from, and supremacy over, na-ture.[78] Clearly, this challenges the outlandish commentators such as Rush Limbaugh who maintain the fanatical position that "[i]f the owl can't adapt to the superiority of humans, then screw it."[79] While our society explores the notion that species are sacred (with intriguing reflections on the Noah story, among others), critics assert that the ESA fails to recognize the "sanctity" of private property,[80] a remarkable, and as yet unexplained, theological position.

THE SOLUTIONS: INTEGRATION OF SCALES

If the conflicts arising between the ESA and private property owners are a function of the values and concerns that arise from different scales of perception, it follows that there may be two means for resolving these conflicts. First, it may be possible to implement the ESA in ways that ex-plicitly take into consideration the small-scale concerns of those who own private property. Second, by increasing the scale at which we per-ceive private property, it may be possible to find the common ground between these lands and the ecosystems upon which all species depend.

Scaling Down the ESA

Although the ESA is, "on the face," a large-scale conceptualization, it is conceivably possible to implement the act with attention to the unique perspectives of the private property owner. Appropriate mechanisms are possible within the constraints of the act, and several prototypes have been developed. Although the administration of these mechanisms is, in some cases, problematic, they provide a compelling set of approaches to closing the gap between the perceptual scales.

The most direct means of recognizing the scale of private property is the Small Landowner Exemption, through which the ESA allows hardship exemptions for individuals.[81] The National Wildlife Federation's Community-based Recovery Planning proposal recommends priority consideration for exempting small, residential property owners from the constraints of the act.[82] In cases where exemptions are infeasible, such private property owners are provided with compensation through tax incentives and direct assistance.[83] The DOI appears to be amenable to such an approach.[84]

The use of public lands as the sites for preservation and recovery is another direct means of shifting the pressure of protecting endangered species from private property. This approach effectively avoids the "tragedy of the commons" by collectivizing both the costs and benefits. According to the DOI, in all cases where appropriate habitats can be found, plans are constructed so that public lands carry the burden of management.[85] Although density transfers and land exchanges may be difficult for small property owners, these indirect means of shifting the burden of the ESA to public lands can also be effective.[86]

The concern of private property owners appears to be, in large part, a function of the perceived "worst case" scenario of confronting the ESA. The fear of private property owners with respect to the ESA has led to the intentional destruction of habitat to prevent colonization by endangered species.[87] As such, proactive implementation via localized planning may reduce the real and perceived risks of future conflicts and avoid the environmental destruction that the act was intended to prevent. In 1982, Congress created a process within the ESA that allowed the incidental taking of threatened and endangered species under the provisions of the habitat conservation plan.[88] (See Chapter 6 for a detailed discussion of HCPs.) In accordance with an HCP, the private property owner is allowed to harm otherwise protected species, as long as such activities do not appreciably diminish the species' survival. Although this mechanism has been criticized because it does not prohibit actions that would diminish a species' *recovery*,[89] it represents a tremendous compromise of the underlying principles of the ESA in deference to the interests of private property owners. Those who would presumably benefit from HCPs are less than enthusiastic about this approach, as it tends to be perceived as expensive and slow. As a result, these plans appear to work better for large rather than small landowners.[90] Recognizing these logistical problems, the DOI advocates the use of federal funds to support HCP development to bring the ESA timescale into concordance with that of private property owners.[91] In addition, the integration of federal agencies involved in implementing the ESA, through a thirteen-agency Memorandum of Understanding,[92] is also intended to accelerate decision making and avoid the regulatory "freeze" that is particularly onerous for small property owners.[93]

Scaling up Private Property

Karr[94] asserts that "[t]hroughout history, the human-environment interaction has generally been significant only at relatively small spatial and temporal scales, [but] Mankind's principal interaction with his environment is no longer at the scale of individuals." Conceptually, we can consider four approaches to expand the scale of private property to close the gap with concerns regarding endangered species. By considering property in the context of incentives, long times, large areas, or complex connections, what is good for humans tends to converge with what is good for other species.

First, the most constructive and potentially powerful means of scaling up perceptions of private property to the ESA is the development of economic incentives, that is, increase the price of ignoring endangered species. Incentives provide a reason for property owners to account for longer time horizons and broader spatial scales. The need to shift the emphasis from punishment to positive reinforcement is probably the most widely endorsed modification of the ESA's implementation, with support coming from the National Wildlife Federation,[95] the Audubon Society,[96] the Environmental Defense Fund,[97] the Interior Department,[98] and the National Wilderness Institute.[99]

An innovative approach to further assuage the concerns of private property owners has been developed and implemented within the broad provisions of the ESA. Rather than having to endure potentially large, future costs of preservation and restoration, some HCPs allow individuals who possess small tracts on which endangered species may depend to "prepay" the costs of mitigation. These fees provide management agencies with necessary funds and provide property owners with a known, up-front cost. For example, a mitigation fee of $600/ac is in effect for the 70,000 ac of the Coachella Valley fringe-toed lizard habitat.[100] In the case of Stephen's Kangaroo rat, the mitigation fee for homebuyers was $215, or less than 0.25 percent of the cost of a new home.[101] This approach straddles the line of compromise between the ESA and private property. From the perspective of the property owner, such mitigation fees may appear to be reverse compensation, but from the collective perspective, the private property owner is charged a small, fixed cost for the privilege of pursuing individual interests that may eventually prevent the recovery of endangered species.

Second, with respect to time, the ESA includes nonprice mechanisms that expand the temporal dimension beyond the lifetime of the private property owner. An HCP can apply to land for decades,[102] allowing a measure of security for both the individual and the species. To balance individual rights with social obligations, perhaps it is valuable to borrow a page from the National Environmental Policy Act, which accepts the environment as a form of property. This property is viewed as a trusteeship with obligations between generations.[103] Species are part of the American heritage, and we can no more justify generating a massive environmental deficit than we can rationalize passing along an excessive monetary debt.[104] In still more familiar terms, conflicts between private property and endangered species would seem to be substantially diminished if we took seriously the notion that the land is not something we inherit from our ancestors but something that we borrow from our children.[105]

Third, in terms of expanding our perceptions of private property along the spatial dimension, it is essential to understand that the American frontier is closed—the option of moving to new lands should the environment become unable to support us is no longer viable.[106] This represents a tremendous change in the manner in which our society perceives property. As noted by Mann and Plummer,[107] "Until recent decades, Americans were untroubled by such questions. The nation was still empty [and] there seemed no need to choose between a species and economic growth. But now the country's empty corners are filling up, and biologists warn that in the next decade or two the fate of thousands of species will be decided."

Again the ESA provides a nonprice means for expanding the spatial scope of the property owner. Regional HCPs cover multiple species across entire landscapes.[108] This approach is cumbersome, as it necessarily involves many people and demands informed community support,[109] but such may be the price of conducting the business of government in a crowded world. Ironically, this approach has been favored by both land developers and environmentalists, with the former being cynically accused of attempting to avoid the ESA and the latter trying to enforce its prohibitions.[110] But given that the potential to act autonomously on our "own land" is an anachronistic luxury, there can be little doubt that "[w]e have to begin to think of ourselves as inhabitants of ecosystems and begin to live, think, and act accordingly."[111]

Finally, it may be possible, and perhaps even necessary, to re-perceive private property in the context of our increasing intensity of connectedness. Rose[112] provided an incisive summary of the private property–ESA conflict in noting that "[e]nvironmentalism is only a particularly pointed example of a recurring problem in free and democratic governments: the importance of self-imposed citizen restraints for the sake of a common good." The DOI has expressly pursued increased community involvement in the development of plans for habitat conservation and species recovery.[113] The NWF has called for the evolution of the HCP procedure into "Community-based Recovery Planning," which fully involves people in the entire process.[114] As difficult as trade-offs between personal and community interests might be to resolve, they are not new or unfamiliar. "Our society has a fundamental premise: Regulatory action taken for a valid public purpose can have consequences that legally inconvenience people and, from time to time, do diminish someone's rights," and in this regard one might view the ESA as an extension of a well-known constraint—planning and zoning laws.[115]

The perception of the species or ecosystems as property, even large-scale or community property, is fiercely resisted by some environmentalists, but the legal and ethical tradition of private property in Western culture is a rich source of ideas for narrowing the gap between species preservation and property rights.[116] Contrary to what has become conventional environmental wisdom, not all commons end in tragedy. Species may be preserved through the same mechanisms that sustain these surviving commons—normative appeals regarding thrift, carefulness, overuse, and sustainability. As noted by Rose,[117] "even individual property revolves around these normative characteristics [of common property]. The indi-

vidual property-holder relies in great part on the recognition and acqui-
escence of others, and individual property law assumes a large measure of
neighborliness and attentiveness to the needs of others in the use of one's
own 'exclusive' property." At its best, the integration of an individual's
private property rights with one's commensurate obligations to the community includes a normative "deep structure" familiar to environmental
ethics.

CONCLUSIONS

In an immediate sense, enlightened self-interest would seem to be a compelling argument for protecting our biological infrastructure. We must
ask whether the richest nation on earth is more desperately in need of
further economic wealth or natural assets.[118] However, it seems that
perhaps something more profound than sophisticated self-interest is at
hand. There appears to be an ongoing national examination of what constitutes "self."

Indigenous people tend to view the world in terms of kinship, with
species being neither untouchable gifts nor exploitable givens.[119] The dis-
tinction between self and other is blurred, such that to harm another is to
harm oneself. As our society is coming to realize that there is no place left
to move and that we are thus tied to land in a way that has not been true
since the rise of Western culture, it appears that we are in the process of
becoming indigenous. Indeed, Leopold's land ethic was in many ways an
ethic of kinship in the tradition of native people; Nature was understood
to be an end in itself, not simply a means to our ends.[120] The development
of this sense of "place" by which our modern society seems to be defining
itself is a difficult, even painful, process. However, the ESA is central to
this struggle, and while its implementation needs ongoing attention, its
principles are sound—the well-being of humans and other species is in-
extricably linked.

NOTES

1   S. A. Levin, The Problem of Pattern and Scale in Ecology, *Ecology* 73(1992):
     1943–1967.
2   T. F. H. Allen and T. W. Hoekstra, *Toward a Unified Ecology* (New York: Colum-
     bia University Press, 1992).

3   M. Kriz, Caught in the Act, *National Journal,* December 1995, 3090–3094.
4   E. Losos, The Future of the U.S. Endangered Species Act, *Trends in Ecology and Evolution* 8(1993):332–336.
5   T. Bethell, Species Logic, *American Spectator* (August 1995):20–22.
6   E. O. Wilson, *Biodiversity* (Washington, D.C.: National Academy Press, 1988).
7   M. Beattie, The Endangered Species Act: Myths and Realities (paper presented at the Society of Environmental Journalists meeting, Los Angeles, 20 May 1995).
8   Wilson, *Biodiversity.*
9   J. M. Patlis, Biodiversity, Ecosystems and Species: Where Does the Endangered Species Act Fit In? *Tulane Environmental Law Journal* 8(1994):33–76.
10 W. Jackson, *New Roots for Agriculture* (Lincoln: University of Nebraska Press, 1980).
11 N. K. Kubasek and M. N. Browne, The Endangered Species Act: An Evaluation of Alternative Approaches, *Dickinson Journal of Environmental Law & Policy* 3(1994):1–18.
12 B. Babbitt, The Endangered Species Act and "Takings": A Call for Innovation within the Terms of the Act, *Environmental Law* 24(1994):355–367.
13 T. H. Watkins, What's Wrong with the Endangered Species Act? *Audubon* (January–February 1996):37–41.
14 Beattie, The Endangered Species Act: Myths and Realities.
    Watkins, What's Wrong with the Endangered Species Act?
15 Information from the Fish and Wildlife Service Internet World Wide Web page at http://www.fws.gov., 1996.
16 Beattie, The Endangered Species Act: Myths and Realities.
17 Fish and Wildlife Service, *Report to Congress: Endangered and Threatened Species Recovery Program* (Washington, D.C.: U.S. Department of the Interior, Fish and Wildlife Service, 1995).
    Watkins, What's Wrong with the Endangered Species Act?
18 Losos, The Future of the U.S. Endangered Species Act.
    Kubasek and Browne, The Endangered Species Act: An Evaluation of Alternative Approaches.
    R. C. Wilson, Triage and the Endangered Species Act, *Transactions of the 60th North American Wildlife and Natural Resources Conference* (1995):463–465.
    National Wildlife Federation, Involving Communities in Conservation: A Policy Position Paper on the Endangered Species Act, 1995, 32 pp.
19 In D. J. Rohlf, Six Biological Reasons Why the Endangered Species Act Doesn't Work—and What to Do about It, *Conservation Biology* 5(1991):273–282.
20 J. B. Ruhl, Regional Habitat Conservation Planning under the Endangered Species Act: Pushing the Legal and Practical Limits of Species Protection, *Land Use and Environmental Law Review* 23(1992):535–567.
21 Rohlf, Six Biological Reasons Why the Endangered Species Act Doesn't Work.
22 Ibid.
23 Wilson, *Biodiversity.*
24 Endangered Species Act, 16 U.S.C. 1531–1544.
25 Kubasek and Browne, The Endangered Species Act: An Evaluation of Alternative Approaches.
26 Wilson, *Biodiversity.*

27 Beattie, The Endangered Species Act: Myths and Realities.
   FWS, *Report to Congress: Endangered and Threatened Species Recovery Program* (1995).
   The misguided assertions of R. E. Gordon (Saving Endangered Species: What's Really Happening? *American Mining Congress Journal* [June 1994]:6–8) and T. Bethell (Species Logic, *American Spectator* [August 1995]:20–22) notwithstanding.
28 Patlis, Biodiversity, Ecosystems and Species.
   O. A. Houck, Reflections on the Endangered Species Act, *Environmental Law* 25(1995):689–702.
29 Ruhl, Regional Habitat Conservation Planning under the Endangered Species Act.
30 Rohlf, Six Biological Reasons Why the Endangered Species Act Doesn't Work.
31 Ibid.
32 Ibid.
   Losos, The Future of the U.S. Endangered Species Act.
33 Patlis, Biodiversity, Ecosystems and Species.
   Ruhl, Regional Habitat Conservation Planning under the Endangered Species Act.
34 Houck, Reflections on the Endangered Species Act.
35 FWS, *Facts about the Endangered Species Act* (Washington, D.C.: U.S. Fish and Wildlife Service, 1995).
36 Ibid.
   Houck, Reflections on the Endangered Species Act.
37 General Accounting Office, *Endangered Species Act: Information on Species Protection on Nonfederal Lands,* GAO/RCED-95-16 (Washington, D.C.: U.S. General Accounting Office, 1994).
38 Losos, The Future of the U.S. Endangered Species Act.
39 FWS, *Facts about the Endangered Species Act.*
40 H. H. Thompson, Administration Proposes Endangered Species Act Exemptions for Small Landowners (U.S. Department of the Interior News Release, 1995).
41 Beattie, The Endangered Species Act: Myths and Realities.
42 Patlis, Biodiversity, Ecosystems and Species.
43 Ibid.
44 Kubasek and Browne, The Endangered Species Act: An Evaluation of Alternative Approaches.
   FWS, *Report to Congress: Endangered and Threatened Species Recovery Program* (1995).
45 FWS, *Report to Congress: Endangered and Threatened Species Recovery Program* (1995).
46 Losos, The Future of the U.S. Endangered Species Act.
47 Allen and Hoekstra, *Toward a Unified Ecology.*
48 Patlis, Biodiversity, Ecosystems and Species.
49 C. C. Mann and M. L. Plummer, The Butterfly Problem, *Atlantic Monthly* (January 1992):47–70.
50 Wilson, *Biodiversity.*

51 See, for example, L. E. Johnson, *A Morally Deep World: An Essay on Moral Significance and Environmental Ethics* (New York: Cambridge University Press, 1991).
Mann and Plummer, The Butterfly Problem.
National Wildlife Federation, Involving Communities in Conservation.

52 National Wildlife Federation, Involving Communities in Conservation.

53 C. M. Rose, Given-ness and Gift: Property and the Quest for Environmental Ethics, *Environmental Law* 24(1994):1–30.

54 J. R. Karr, Biological Integrity and the Goal of Environmental Legislation: Lessons for Conservation Biology, *Conservation Biology* 4(1990):244–250.
Losos, The Future of the U.S. Endangered Species Act.

55 Beattie, The Endangered Species Act: Myths and Realities.

56 Wilson, Triage and the Endangered Species Act.

57 Beattie, The Endangered Species Act: Myths and Realities.

58 Mann and Plummer, The Butterfly Problem.
Wilson, Triage and the Endangered Species Act.

59 Losos, The Future of the U.S. Endangered Species Act.

60 Babbitt, The Endangered Species Act and "Takings."

61 Rohlf, Six Biological Reasons Why the Endangered Species Act Doesn't Work.
Losos, The Future of the U.S. Endangered Species Act.

62 Mann and Plummer, The Butterfly Problem.
Rose, Given-ness and Gift.

63 Kubasek and Browne, The Endangered Species Act: An Evaluation of Alternative Approaches.

64 Mann and Plummer, The Butterfly Problem.
Wilson, Triage and the Endangered Species Act.

65 Houck, Reflections on the Endangered Species Act.

66 ESA, 16 U.S.C. 1531–1544.

67 For example, see Gordon, Saving Endangered Species: What's Really Happening? for a particularly perplexing presentation.

68 Watkins, What's Wrong with the Endangered Species Act?

69 Ruhl, Regional Habitat Conservation Planning under the Endangered Species Act.

70 Watkins, What's Wrong with the Endangered Species Act?
National Wildlife Federation, Involving Communities in Conservation.

71 Kubasek and Browne, The Endangered Species Act: An Evaluation of Alternative Approaches.

72 Losos, The Future of the U.S. Endangered Species Act.

73 J. R. Stoll and L. E. Johnson, Concepts of Value, Nonmarket Valuation, and the Case of the Whooping Crane, *Transactions of the North American Wildlife and Natural Resources Conference* 49(1984):382–393.

74 See Johnson, *A Morally Deep World,* for a particularly well-conceived and rigorous analysis of the intrinsic value of species from the perspective of well-being interests.

75 Mann and Plummer, The Butterfly Problem.

76 Ruhl, Regional Habitat Conservation Planning under the Endangered Species Act.

77   Kubasek and Browne, The Endangered Species Act: An Evaluation of Alternative Approaches.

78   Wilson, Triage and the Endangered Species Act.

79   In Beattie, The Endangered Species Act: Myths and Realities.

80   Kriz, Caught in the Act.

81   ESA, 16 U.S.C. 1531–1544.
         FWS, *Report to Congress: Endangered and Threatened Species Recovery Program* (1995).

82   National Wildlife Federation, Involving Communities in Conservation.

83   Ibid.

84   Thompson, Administration Proposes Endangered Species Act Exemptions for Small Landowners.

85   Babbitt, The Endangered Species Act and "Takings."

86   Ibid.

87   Kriz, Caught in the Act.

88   Mann and Plummer, The Butterfly Problem.
         FWS, *Report to Congress: Endangered and Threatened Species Recovery Program* (1995).

89   Rohlf, Six Biological Reasons Why the Endangered Species Act Doesn't Work.
         Babbitt, The Endangered Species Act and "Takings."

90   FWS, *Facts about the Endangered Species Act.*

91   Babbitt, The Endangered Species Act and "Takings."

92   Patlis, Biodiversity, Ecosystems and Species.

93   Babbitt, The Endangered Species Act and "Takings."

94   Karr, Biological Integrity and the Goal of Environmental Legislation.

95   National Wildlife Federation, Involving Communities in Conservation.

96   Watkins, What's Wrong with the Endangered Species Act?

97   Kriz, Caught in the Act.

98   Thompson, Administration Proposes Endangered Species Act Exemptions for Small Landowners.

99   Gordon, Saving Endangered Species: What's Really Happening?

100 FWS, *Report to Congress: Endangered and Threatened Species Recovery Program* (1995).

101 Ibid.

102 FWS, *Report to Congress: Endangered and Threatened Species Recovery Program* (1995).

103 Rose, Given-ness and Gift.

104 Watkins, What's Wrong with the Endangered Species Act?
         National Wildlife Federation, Involving Communities in Conservation.

105 Rose, Given-ness and Gift.

106 Ibid.
         Karr, Biological Integrity and the Goal of Environmental Legislation.

107 Mann and Plummer, The Butterfly Problem.

108 Kubasek and Browne, The Endangered Species Act: An Evaluation of Alternative Approaches.
         FWS, *Report to Congress: Endangered and Threatened Species Recovery Program* (1995).

109 Ruhl, Regional Habitat Conservation Planning under the Endangered Species Act.
110 Ibid.
111 Babbitt, The Endangered Species Act and "Takings."
112 Rose, Given-ness and Gift.
113 FWS, *Report to Congress: Endangered and Threatened Species Recovery Program* (1995).
114 National Wildlife Federation, Involving Communities in Conservation.
115 Babbitt, The Endangered Species Act and "Takings."
116 Rose, Given-ness and Gift.
117 Ibid.
118 Thompson, Administration Proposes Endangered Species Act Exemptions for Small Landowners.
119 Rose, Given-ness and Gift.
120 Ibid.

⁂ 6 ⁂

The Private Lands Challenge: Integrating Biodiversity Conservation and Private Property

John F. Turner and Jason C. Rylander

A Wyoming wind sent waves out across the rolling grasslands of Shirley Basin. A small crowd had gathered on that day in 1992 to witness the reintroduction of the world's rarest mammal—the elusive and beautiful black-footed ferret—to its historic range. The isolated area chosen for the release of the first "nonessential experimental population" of ferrets was on private property in the heart of cattle country, where livestock pastures maintained an enviable habitat of prairie dog towns and grazed grass communities.

At the time, I (Turner) was director of the U.S. Fish and Wildlife Service and thus responsible for the administration of the endangered species program. I thanked one of the young ranchers for being a willing partner in this risky but exciting experiment. Looking out across the lush rolling hills of his ranch, he grinned and said, "John, please don't brag on this to my friends at the Wyoming Stock Growers Convention, but the family and I are really enjoying this project. We are excited about bringing this critter back to our country, and we're proud to have our ranch part of this experiment."

For several months, Wyoming had been the center of controversy over the Endangered Species Act. Livestock groups were blasting the FWS, the ESA, and me as director, for our plan to return wolves to the Yellowstone region. The prevailing sentiment was that "neither the Act nor the federal bureaucrats can be trusted." Yet for weeks, this rancher and his neighbors had tolerated a progression of state and federal biologists tramping over their property surveying the land, setting up observation posts, laying transects, plotting release and management areas, and coordinating the actual release. The ESA gave us no authority to be there, but these folks had agreed to be our partners strictly on a voluntary basis.

At first there were many questions. What if, in the future, a rancher accidentally baled a ferret while putting up his winter hay? Or what if his cow dog killed one of the rare animals while working cattle? Would a federal agent arrive some day and shut down his operation to protect the ferrets? These folks lived in the heart of "wise use" country and were justifiably cautious. Yet, once they realized that the ESA was flexible enough to provide binding assurances that they would be exempt from liability for any incidental harm to the ferrets or their habitat, these ranchers were glad to participate in the recovery effort.

If such a partnership could be forged on the plains of central Wyoming, why is there such a storm raging across America over the ESA and its impact on private property? In my tenure with the FWS, we fashioned thousands of voluntary partnerships with farmers, ranchers, developers, and timber companies to protect listed species, wetlands, and other habitat, yet property rights concerns have erupted in recent months, dominating discussions of the ESA. The debate is characterized by a swirl of accusations, misconceptions, and alleged horror stories of private landowners suffering impacts because of the "long arm" of this law. Critics of the act have raised valid issues that should be addressed in the reauthorization of this statute. The havoc wreaked across communities in the name of species protection, however, is overstated. Many of the "horror stories" are difficult to substantiate. Most such anecdotes are intended to undermine public support for the ESA and convince lawmakers to weaken the statute to promote specific economic interests.

The land ethic is strong in this country, as is our commitment to private property rights. As De Tocqueville noted more than one hundred years ago, "In no country in the world is the love of property more active and more anxious than in the United States; nowhere does the majority display less inclination for those principles which threaten to alter, in whatever manner, the laws of property."[1] Attempts to pit conservation against property rights can only serve to undermine both principles.

In part, the conflict arises because the ESA is being asked to do too much. Our living resource legacy is eroding because federal, state, local, and even private stewardship initiatives have failed to keep pace with the loss of suitable habitat in this country. By the time the ESA comes into play, it is almost too late. The species is already on the brink of extinction, and efforts to save what few specimens remain inevitably impact disproportionately the lands where the species still exists. Most property owners want to do the right thing, but they feel they are bearing too much of the burden of protection simply because they happen to own the majority of the nation's remaining wetlands, riparian corridors, and endangered species habitat.

Landowners have every right to be proud of their general stewardship across the United States. Preliminary information presented by Michael Bean, endangered species expert for the Environmental Defense Fund, however, would seem to show that declining wildlife populations are not doing well on private property.[2] For listed species that are found entirely on federal lands, about 18 percent seem to be improving and 39 percent are stable in status.[3] However, notes Bean, for those that are found on private property, only 3 percent are improving and only 16 percent are thought to be stable.[4] He uses as an example the serious decline of the Attwater's prairie chicken (*Tympanuchus cupido*), which depends upon private lands for its existence. "Its wild population has fallen from over 2,250 in 1975 to only 42 in 1996. Indeed, its population has declined by over 90 percent in the three years since 1993."[5] These observations illustrate that we need better strategies to protect rarer species on private property.

We must all work to find positive and proactive mechanisms to encourage the nation's landowners to embrace the protection and enhancement of natural resources on private lands. At the same time, reasonable standards must be kept in place to protect the nation's water, land productivity, and living resources to thwart those who would disregard such responsibilities. We must also respect the communities and lifestyles that have helped shape the land. This is our wildlife conservation challenge for this decade and the next century. As René Dubos noted: "Ecology becomes a more complex but far more interesting science when human aspirations are regarded as an integral part of the landscape."[6]

This chapter discusses the implementation of approaches under the current ESA that are proving successful in establishing positive partnerships between property owners and species conservationists. Many of these approaches, such as the increased use of habitat conservation plans with incidental take permits, increased involvement of private landowners in the recovery of species, conservation agreements, prelisting activities, and safe harbor rules, were conceived or more broadly applied during the Bush administration. These and other approaches have been embraced and expanded by Interior Secretary Bruce Babbitt and the Clinton administration. Several bills have been introduced in Congress to reauthorize the ESA since it came due in 1992, but none of these efforts has been successful. The relationship of private property owners to conserving endangered species has been central to the reauthorization debate.

If species conservation on private land is to be successful, programs outside the ESA must also be supported. In addition to examining key provisions of the ESA, this chapter will highlight a number of model programs that are already providing assistance and incentives to landowners who embrace the protection of species and habitat.

All levels of government have a role to play in the conservation of the nation's natural resource heritage. Partnerships between public, private, and nonprofit interests represent the future of conservation. Yaffee[7] writes: "Endangered species management is as much about organizing and dealing with humans and human institutions as it is about dealing with plants and animals. The success of future efforts to protect biological diversity will depend in large part on how well agencies and professionals understand and act within this sociopolitical context." Working together, it is possible not only to reduce the level of acrimony that now pervades the endangered species debate but also to establish a conservation legacy of which we and our descendants can justly be proud.

EXISTING PROVISIONS THAT AFFECT PROPERTY OWNERS

Prelisting Activities

Having a species targeted with special concerns—either under a state category, as a candidate species for listing under the ESA, or even as a species proposed for a threatened or endangered designation—can prompt collaborative actions that can impact or even preempt possible regulatory actions. Actual ESA listings can be avoided or postponed, or special allowances can be built into a designation, if collective actions to conserve or restore habitat can be agreed upon before a listing becomes necessary. Such mitigating actions must be determined to substantially remove impacts that threaten species survival. Current ESA provisions allow such flexibility, and the following models demonstrate that prelisting efforts can accommodate species protection *and* landowner concerns.

CASE STUDY: LOUISIANA BLACK BEAR

In June 1990, the FWS received a petition to list the Louisiana black bear (*Ursus americanus luteolus*) as threatened based on human exploitation and extensive loss of habitat. The bear ranged throughout Louisiana, in two-thirds of Mississippi, and in east Texas, with nearly 90 percent of its habitat found on private lands.

Landowners and the forest products industry immediately feared that a potential listing would severely limit or even curtail timber harvesting, which contributed greatly to the economies of local communities and the region. On 14 July 1990, the Louisiana Forestry Association hosted a meeting of concerned individuals from the tristate region. An international authority on black bears, Dr. Michael Pelton, suggested to the gathering that the survival of the bear would depend on the concerted and coordinated effort of diverse public and private interests.

A group of individuals representing a variety of interests quickly came together and formed what became known as the Black Bear Conservation Committee. Eighteen individuals representing timber companies, landowners, conservation groups, and state and federal agencies agreed to check their individual agendas at the door, respect each stakeholder's role and objectives, treat one another as equal partners, and try to work together on behalf of the bears.

The BBCC agreed to work together as public/private partners to accomplish two overriding goals: (1) to stabilize the existing bear population and (2) to attempt to restore bears to suitable habitat within the tristate region where it could eventually be delisted. Biologists from the FWS looked at the best available science and determined that the long-term habitat needs of the bear were compatible with the normal forest management practices of the region.

The efforts of the BBCC reduced the imminent threat to the bear's survival, allowing the FWS to delay listing to give the group time to work out a solution. When listing became necessary, the rule included a provision exempting any incidental take of the species resulting from normal harvesting activities.

An expanded BBCC continued to operate as members understood that the interests of private property could be reconciled in harmony with long-term plans to benefit the threatened species. In sorting out issues and opportunities, the BBCC focuses on habitat, management, education, research, and funding. They have agreed that science will be the final arbiter for their proceedings. The group has produced a management handbook to assist landowners as well as a protocol for handling problem bears. A public awareness campaign has been launched to promote the black bear as an asset, especially for private property owners. The group is finalizing a comprehensive restoration plan that will provide the ingredients of the FWS's draft recovery plan.

All participants of BBCC agree that a worthwhile balance between economic goals and the stewardship responsibility of private lands has been achieved. The resource has benefited and private sector activities have continued. Some basic elements of the BBCC experience are worth noting:

- The Louisiana black bear was an indicator species in a broad hardwood bottomland complex, and its conservation benefits multiple species.
- Diverse local and regional stakeholders, including the affected landowners, led the initiative.
- Organizational agendas were put aside.
- All participants were received with mutual respect and treated as equal partners.
- Everyone signed an agreement recognizing that the well-being of the targeted species was paramount and that all decisions must be based on sound science.
- Incentives were found to make the species compatible with affected landowners.
- The FWS provided the committee with initial coordination and research resources.

The BBCC effort with the Louisiana black bear is an early model of the type of efforts to protect species from endangerment that can be encouraged and even enhanced in the ESA process. Under current law, the ESA has no authority over species that are not threatened or endangered, but actions to prevent species decline, entered into voluntarily with private property owners, are clearly within the scope and intent of the act. More funding, information, and administrative resources could be made avail-

able by the FWS to encourage such collaborative initiatives and local efforts. Listing timetables could be suspended if such groups are observed
to be making measurable progress.

The FWS is currently exploring ways to fashion more official prelisting
agreements that would protect the interests of species and offer long-term
certainty to landowners. Under this approach, landowners concerned
about the future impacts of potential listings could sit down with the FWS,
develop a conservation strategy, and sign an agreement that would protect
their operations from regulation in the event that a species is listed. Species would benefit from the proactive measures landowners would agree
to perform to increase their numbers before a listing crisis occurs. Landowners would likewise benefit from the certainty that regulatory sanctions
would not come into play if the species ultimately is listed.

Specific incentives for landowners should be developed and made
available for such cooperative approaches. The maintenance and restoration of defined habitat on private lands could be further encouraged
through incentives like the Conservation Reserve Program and Wetlands
Reserve Program found in the reauthorized Farm Bill.

Habitat Conservation Plans

Section 10 of the ESA provides for the issuance of an incidental take permit allowing the "take" of a federally listed species if the taking will be
incidental to, and not the purpose of, otherwise legal activities. This flexible provision of the ESA is intended to reduce conflicts and promote creative conservation partnerships between the private sector and government agencies. These partnerships are usually established at the local level
to allow specific development activities that might harm a listed species
in return for voluntary conservation efforts that a permittee will implement to benefit a species or multiple species.

The FWS has only recently begun to explore the full potential of habitat conservation planning. In 1989, at the start of the Bush administration,
only about a half dozen HCPs were under way across the country. Most of
these had been initiated by private parties, and the FWS was only a passive
player. Determined to make the process more widespread and the FWS a
proactive partner in initiating these partnerships, the administration directed considerably more attention to this provision of the ESA. Given that
much of the remaining habitat for listed species was on private lands,
more proactive and voluntary collaboration would have a positive net effect on protection and recovery.

The agency convened diverse interests involved with ESA issues at the local level, explained HCP opportunities, offered technical and biological assistance, and then reviewed plans. Approximately 100 HCP projects were in some stage of development in June 1993. The Clinton administration has continued this emphasis with the commitment of additional resources, and the number of HCP projects under way continues to expand. As of April 1996, there were 131 HCPs in place and another 200 in development.[8]

HCP projects can vary greatly in scope. In Florida's Brevard County, 0.5-acre to 9-acre incidental take permits have been issued for HCPs to conserve habitat for the Florida scrub jay (*Aphelocoma coerulescens coerulus*).[9] A much larger, 450,000-acre plan is being developed with International Paper Company in Alabama and Mississippi to protect the gopher tortoise (*Gopherus polyphemus*).[10] As director of the FWS, in 1992 I signed the first HCP effort for the northern spotted owl (*Strix occidentalis caurina*) with Simpson Lumber Co. to provide an increased flow of timber and the conservation of owls on 380,000 acres in northern California.[11] Another 30,000-acre HCP with International Paper was permitted in 1993 to allow sustainable timber harvests and also protect critical habitat for the red-hills salamander (*Phaeognathus hubrichti*) in Alabama. This agreement also addressed watershed-quality goals by protecting habitat on slopes of more than 30 percent, where clear-cutting was expensive and likely to cause increased sedimentation.

Although most HCPs are designed to address the decline of a single species, many target and render multispecies benefits. Certainly one of the most challenging HCP efforts involves the 6,000-square-mile conservation planning area between Los Angeles and Mexico in southern California.

This region hosts nearly half of the state's residents, some of the most expensive real estate in the country, and a once biologically rich landscape under siege. Development and agriculture had already consumed 70 to 90 percent of the region's coastal sage scrub habitat.[12] Nearly one hundred individual species—including the coastal cactus wren, California Mastiff bat, Hermes copper butterfly, orange-throated whiptail, black sage, prickly pear cactus, and the California buckwheat—were already classified as rare or in some degree of peril by federal and state resource agencies.[13]

Political values in this contentious California atmosphere included resistance to new taxes, high regard for property rights, and a deep appreciation for natural areas and wildlife. Developers, county officials, and environmental interests had been engaged in a piecemeal approach that was costly and bitter, with little benefit to dwindling populations of natural resources. Governor Pete Wilson, Natural Resource Secretary Doug Wheeler, and leaders of the FWS were determined to attempt a bold scheme of compromise that could induce landowners and local officials to protect blocks of remaining habitat and corridors for multiple species while in turn releasing other areas needed for development. What emerged was the Natural Community Conservation Planning effort.[14]

With the listing of the California gnatcatcher (*Polioptila californica californica*), the FWS became a partner in the NCCP process. This high-risk and bold effort was an attempt to begin a multispecies, multi-interest partnership to get beyond the tract-by-tract, species-by-species, "white hat—black hat" warfare that had characterized species protection efforts in the area.[15]

Advisory panels and scientists have struggled with negotiations to reach compromises in Orange, San Diego, and Riverside Counties. Mega-landowners like the Irvine Company have signed on as willing partners. A 39,000-acre preserve in central and coastal Orange County is currently under consideration, and agreement on a 150,000-acre preserve in the greater San Diego area is expected soon.[16] Mainstream environmental groups, reasonable developers, and government agencies have made progress, while radical environmental groups and extreme property rights advocates have been marginalized. Some developers have realized that the pre-NCCP times resulted in costly impasses and that the set-aside conservation areas can greatly enhance real estate values where development is permitted.[17]

The use of the HCP and ITP provisions has increased dramatically around the United States in recent years. HCP efforts currently under way include:[18]

Georgia—1,000,000 acres	Florida—10,000 acres
South Carolina—3,000,000 acres	Texas—633,000 acres
Mississippi—500,000 acres	Washington—3,000,000 acres
Oregon—300,000 acres	Utah—135,000 acres

CASE STUDY: "SAFE HARBORS" AND RED-COCKADED WOODPECKERS

One recent example of the flexibility and innovative potential that already exists in the ESA is the "safe harbors" program announced by the FWS in

March 1995.[19] The idea was simple. If landowners would permit threatened and endangered species to nest on their property and agree to manage their lands to promote habitat enhancement, the FWS would assure them that they would not be penalized or restricted from converting their land to other uses at a later date.

The model for the now nationwide safe harbors plan is officially known as the North Carolina Sandhills Habitat Conservation Plan, which was developed to encourage voluntary restoration and enhancement of red-cockaded woodpecker (*Picoides borealis*) habitat by private landowners. Currently, 4,694 pairs of red-cockaded woodpeckers (RCWs) are known to exist in thirteen southeastern states. The bird's preferred habitat, long-leaf pine forests, once covered 92 million acres of the south but now totals less than 4 million acres. The bird was declared an endangered species in 1970. The North Carolina Sandhills population is one of fifteen populations considered critical to the recovery of the species. Although much of the bird's remaining habitat is found on public lands, roughly 21 percent of the birds reside on private property.[20]

The groundwork for the plan was laid in September 1992, when the FWS and the U.S. Army cohosted a meeting of various agencies and organizations at Fort Bragg, N.C., to develop an overall conservation strategy for the woodpecker.[21] Subsequent working groups involving agency biologists, army representatives, state and local officials, academics, and conservation groups continued work on the plan. Under Section 7 of the ESA, which requires that all federal agencies consult with the FWS before engaging in any activities that may affect species or their habitat, the U.S. Army would have to make sure its activities at Fort Bragg were not detrimental to the woodpecker. In response to the army's concerns, and with their assistance and cooperation, all efforts were made to ensure that RCW protection efforts would be compatible with military training and readiness activities.

The overriding challenge in fashioning a management strategy was to conserve older longleaf habitat in the Sandhills region not only for RCW populations but also for a dozen other listed species and some forty candidate species, including the bald eagle (*Haliaeetus leucocephalus*) and peregrine falcon (*Falco francisis*). As of 1990, only 7 percent of pine plantations in North Carolina had stands more than thirty years old. Only a fraction of 1 percent were over forty years old.[22] The forest products industry, the third largest component of the state's economy, employing over 100,000 workers, promoted harvest rotation cycles too short to allow the growth of older trees adequate for woodpecker nests and cavities. In addition, forest composition changed as growers turned away from long-leaf to loblolly pine (*Pinus taeda*) and slash pine (*Pinus ellotii*) forests, which have a shorter rotation cycle. Fire suppression permitted the encroachment of hardwood understory that was detrimental to the RCW's longleaf habitat. Forests were being fragmented by agriculture and urban growth.

Developed in response to widespread fears that the presence of RCWs on private lands would lead to sweeping land-use restrictions, safe harbors offer landowners favorable alternatives. Reports of landowners clearing habitat to prevent RCWs from getting established on their land were growing more common (though actual incidents were probably overstated), so the first step was to remove the disincentives for woodpecker protection.

The plan was the first of its kind in a number of ways. First, while habitat conservation plans are generally developed to mitigate or offset planned development impacts, the safe harbor initiative was designed to encourage proactive, voluntary habitat improvements in advance of specific threats to the species. Second, this was the first time the FWS applied for and received its own Section 10(a)(1) incidental take permit to implement the plan.

The name "safe harbors" is credited to Marsh Smith, a member of the Sandhills Area Land Trust, a grassroots organization devoted to woodland conservation. Michael Bean, who was already looking at incentive-based ways to protect species, analyzed a variety of approaches to implement it on private lands across the region. Bean and FWS biologists Janice Nicholls and Mark Cantrell drafted the HCP, and it was formally proposed in February 1995.[23]

Since its inception, the safe harbors plan has been touted as a model for species conservation around the country and landowner interest has been significant. As of the end of 1997, twenty-four landowners, with over 24,000 acres, had signed agreements to participate in the program. The first to sign up was the Pinehurst Resort and Country Club, which, like many of the other landowners participating in the program, has taken great pride in working with the FWS to protect birds. As a result of their agreement, they can rest assured that no regulatory hammer will come crashing down on them. Landowners also receive a certificate of participation from the FWS and community recognition of their work for species.

In fiscal year 1995, the FWS also provided $16,000 in funding assistance under the Partners for Wildlife program to enhance approximately two thousand acres of habitat for twenty-three RCW groups on four privately owned properties in the Sandhills. "[Safe harbors] is opening eyes to how living with an endangered species is not difficult and in fact is pretty neat," said Cantrell. "More people are becoming proud that they do provide habitat for endangered species. It's something that they can take ownership in. Landowners are much more open to listen if it's a suggestion rather than a demand. Now I've got people calling and asking if I can come and drill [woodpecker] cavities on their land."[24]

Safe harbors is a relatively easy way for smaller landowners to participate in woodpecker recovery, and gain economic certainty, without having to negotiate individual HCPs, as larger industrial landowners have done. When safe harbors was announced, the FWS had already approved memorandums of understanding with Georgia-Pacific Corp., Hancock Timber Resource Group, and Champion International and had additional plans under negotiation.[25]

"It is very important that folks realize that this may not work for every species; it's just one of the creative ideas that you can come up with under the present act," Nicholls said. "The HCP process is wide open, and it takes creative minds especially from the private sector to say, 'Hey, why don't we try this?'"[26]

In addition, the woodpecker HCP contained a "no surprises" policy, signed by Secretary Babbitt on 11 August 1994, which assured participating landowners that the FWS would not place additional restrictions on them unless they agreed to them or unless the landowners breached the agreement. The benefits to the timber products industry and other landowners are obvious. In addition, landscapers are becoming attracted to the availability of hardwood plants in understory communities. Greenhouses are finding new outlets for longleaf pine seedlings. Even the Sandhills Chamber of Commerce has created a task force to promote conserving and growing natural vegetation like longleaf in areas facing economic and urban development.[27]

The experience of safe harbors and habitat conservation planning in North Carolina and the southeastern region offers many examples of how the ESA can work with landowners to achieve economic and environmental goals. Of course, the process can be improved. In an attempt to minimize costs, paperwork, and administrative delay and oversight of small landowners with woodpecker populations, the FWS is proposing the development of statewide HCPs. Such a plan would include all qualified landowners under a statewide incidental take permit held by the state wildlife or forestry agency. Instead of negotiating fifty HCPs for as many landowners with similar management needs, one would suffice. The FWS is working with the states of Georgia, South Carolina, and Alabama to develop statewide plans.

In 1997 the FWS and NMFS announced a Draft Safe Harbor Policy under the ESA [28] and a proposed rule to codify the substance of the safe harbor policy [29] and the "no surprises" policy. [30] These steps acknowledge that the involvement of the private sector is critical to the success of species conservation and recovery.

Conservation Agreements

A conservation agreement is another tool to protect species while offering flexibility to private landowners. Similar to prelisting agreements, conservation agreements are voluntary commitments between the FWS and individuals or organizations designed to protect species that are listed as threatened or endangered, proposed for listing, or candidates for listing. The agreements often take the form of management plans. Frequently, they document the specific actions and responsibilities that each party agrees to in attempting to conserve the targeted species and its habitat.

Unlike HCPs, conservation agreements do not provide for the incidental take of a listed species. If proposed activities are deemed likely to result in incidental take, the property owner must still apply for a permit and may choose to enter into a formal HCP. Also, conservation agreements are usually targeted to address the needs of a single species. As a result, the process can be faster and more flexible than developing an HCP. The process is dynamic in that private and public parties usually agree to continue working together on actual management plans, research, and changing stipulations.

The potential role of conservation agreements in prelisting conservation efforts was recognized in 1997 with the announcement by the FWS and NMFS of a draft policy [31] and proposed rule [32] for candidate conservation agreements. The policy's objective is to conserve proposed, candidate, and certain other unlisted species on private lands, while providing long-term regulatory assurances to the participating landowners. Overall, conservation agreements are excellent mechanisms for public/

private partnerships in reaching a balance between sustainable economic activities and the protection and enhancement of species.

CASE STUDIES: CONSERVATION AGREEMENTS

Swan Valley, Montana. Plum Creek Timber Company is the nation's largest private landowner of habitat for the threatened silvertip grizzly bear (*Ursus arctos*). Aside from its holdings in Washington and Idaho, the integrated timber products company owns 200,000 acres in western Montana's Swan Valley. These lands are intermingled in a checkerboard fashion with adjacent lands under the control of the Flathead National Forest, Montana's Division of State Lands, and smaller landowners.

Plum Creek's ability to access its private timber was often dependent upon the approval of the governmental agencies to allow road construction and access across public lands. Approval was often delayed for years because of concerns about impacts on the area's remaining grizzlies. The bear requires large areas of habitat where road densities and use are low enough to minimize human-caused mortalities. In addition, biologists were concerned that further habitat degradation in the Swan Valley could isolate the Mission Mountain grizzlies from important habitat in the Bob Marshall Wilderness Area nearby.

New road building on national forest lands to meet Plum Creek's needs would likely have exceeded density guidelines established by the Interagency Grizzly Bear Committee. If such fears were valid, any national forest plans for new roads across public lands to allow the company to access their private lands would have constituted a federal action subject to a Section 7 review by the FWS.

Recall that all federal actions that potentially threaten the survival of listed species must be reviewed under Section 7 of the ESA. Such proposed actions are subject to consultation between the action agency and the FWS or the NMFS. If a "jeopardy" opinion is issued, the potential action must be revised. On rare occasions, the proposed actions are rescinded or delayed indefinitely. A landowner whose activities depend on federal actions, such as road building, can be impacted accordingly. To avoid the need for a Section 7 ruling or minimize the likelihood that their activities may harm a species, landowners can sometimes enter into conservation agreements to protect their interests. By participating in a proactive consensus-building process, Plum Creek fashioned a "win-win" solution for the company and the bears.

A conservation agreement was signed by all the principal parties and announced on 18 December 1995.[33] Covering nearly 370,000 acres of Swan Valley, the agreement will (1) mitigate impacts of existing and new roads for timber access, (2) allow Plum Creek to proceed with timbering activities, (3) provide conservation measures that will enhance grizzly bear recovery in Swan Valley, (4) comply with the ESA, (5) establish "best management practices" for future harvesting, and (6) give some assurance of future relief from ESA restrictions.

Low-elevation riparian areas are critical to grizzlies in the spring, yet in Swan Valley these areas are already heavily crisscrossed with roads. Under the plan, spring use of the roads will be severely restricted. Road densities will be higher than IGBC standards, but uses and closures will be agreed upon to benefit the bears. Eleven bear-management "subunits" have been designated for the entire conservation plan area. The company has agreed to rotate harvest schedules among the subunits in a manner that leaves seven of the eleven subunits inactive at any given time for periods of at least three consecutive years. Visual screen cover will be maintained throughout all the subunits. Four "linkage zones" providing migrating corridors across the valley are also established to prevent isolation of the Mission Mountains population. In addition, biologists from Plum Creek and the government agencies are working cooperatively on research and monitoring to ensure that the plan is consistent with species' needs.[34]

Properly conducted logging is usually not a problem for grizzly recovery as long as road use and density are managed to balance the needs of the threatened species with the needs of commercial operations and the public. The Plum Creek agreement seems to strike this balance. Since no harm is expected to befall grizzly populations, provided the agreement is properly carried out, Plum Creek and the Forest Service did not have to apply for an incidental take permit. Charlie Grenier, executive vice-president of Plum Creek, states, "In return for additional protections for the grizzly bear, Plum Creek gains the operational flexibility and regulatory predictability we need to continue to manage our lands." Joel Holtrop, supervisor of the Flathead National Forest, agreed: "This is a win-win situation for all parties . . . We believe this process can be held up as an excellent example of neighbors working together."[35]

Cameron County, Texas. Areas rich in agricultural production are often ripe for ESA clashes. Cameron County's lifeblood is the production and processing of cotton, but the county also hosts six endangered species, including the endangered northern aplomado falcon (*Falco femoralis septentrionalis*).

Following an initial FWS recommendation, the Environmental Protection Agency issued a draft proposal in October 1987 to ban the use of seventeen pesticides in an effort to protect the aplomado falcon. The ban was to be implemented on 1 February 1988, just before the annual cotton planting season. Agricultural interests predicted that the ban would cost the county's economy $125–$350 million per year. Nearly one thousand growers rallied, applied political pressure, and were successful in getting the proposed ban temporarily shelved.

Agricultural leaders, however, worried about their ability to succeed in a prolonged battle with environmental groups and regulators. Four of them gathered to discuss the possibilities of a local group of diverse interests working together toward a successful compromise. Determined to attempt such a collaborative process, those at the lunch meeting literally drafted a mission statement on a table napkin. They agreed on a goal "to address problems and conflicts related to implementing the ESA in Cameron County and to develop and offer functional solutions to the regulatory agencies that will promote compliance with the law and allow the coexistence of endangered species and the agricultural interest in Cameron County to the greatest possible extent."[36]

In March 1988, a nine-member Coexistence Committee was formed and comprised of three growers; the agricultural county extension agent; an agrochemical dealer; one representative each from the Texas Department of Agriculture, Texas Parks and Wildlife Department, and the FWS; and an environmentalist from a county environmental review board. The group sought and received official status as an ad hoc group of county government.

The committee began their deliberations by redefining the problem, building levels of mutual trust, and trying to learn as much as possible about each other's concerns and needs. They pooled all available information and science about farming practices, cotton, atmospheric conditions, and the biology of the northern aplomado falcon. The committee focused on locally based solutions and found that their views were not mutually exclusive. Surprisingly, they reached an early consensus: no one fully supported banning all seventeen pesticides in the county, because it was inappropriate for local conditions.

After several months of work, the growers and environmental groups agreed to a compromise: five chemicals should be banned; another seven could be used; soil applications should be changed for three; and before using two other chemicals, farmers would give the FWS notice. Also, they felt their approach should be applied only in portions of the county that provide suitable habitat for the falcon.

The committee submitted its recommendations to the EPA, but for several months heard nothing. Believing that the EPA was ignoring their compromise, environmental leaders and the FWS called upon the EPA to adopt the solution formulated at the local level. Both regulators and Texas agricultural interests were impressed that the group was able to reach agreement where none had been thought possible. The EPA's original position was reversed, and the FWS issued a "no jeopardy" ruling. The local group later received a stewardship award from the FWS for their innovative and collaborative community problem solving under the ESA.

While this example is not a conservation agreement per se, it is a good example of the kind of proactive local initiatives that the ESA allows. Through local, diverse interests working together, an agreement was reached that provided for both species protection and viable farming activities. With such a management framework in place, the need for further regulation was avoided.

A REVIEW OF PENDING LEGISLATION

Since 1992, Congress has been grappling with ways to amend and reauthorize the ESA. Although a variety of bills were introduced in both the 103d and 104th Congresses, some of which would have dramatically rewritten the ESA, none garnered enough support to win approval in either house of Congress.

A survey of the legislation that has been proposed suggests the emergence of two very different approaches to dealing with the ESA and with landowners' concerns. One approach considers the act basically sound and strives to address complaints by fine-tuning existing provisions and offering incentives for species protection.[37] The other approach would overhaul the ESA's regulatory structure and address landowners' concerns primarily by limiting the reach of the ESA on private lands and providing compensation when problems arise.[38] Which approach, or combination of approaches, will ultimately be chosen remains to be seen. House and Senate leaders face the daunting task of fashioning a bill with bipartisan support that the president will sign. Congress must walk an even tighter rope to balance the often opposing concerns of environmental and industry groups. In the current polarized atmosphere, such a compromise has proven elusive.

It is illustrative to note the different approaches that have been suggested to reform the ESA. Many of the bills have contained thoughtful provisions that may well be included in final legislation. If recent history is a guide, however, it may yet be a long road to consensus on the ESA. The following is a brief analysis of some of the issues before Congress and the provisions in proposed legislation that relate directly to private landowners.

Habitat Protection

THE ISSUE

Much has been written about the extent to which Congress intended to protect species habitat when it passed the ESA in 1973, but it is clear that its authors understood the link between species and habitat. Section 2(b) states that one of the purposes of the ESA is "to provide a means whereby the ecosystems upon which endangered species and threatened species depend may be conserved." The linkage is critical, because research continues to demonstrate that species survival depends on the availability of suitable habitat.[39] The Supreme Court, in the *Sweet Home* case, upheld the FWS's position that the definition of "harm" in the ESA includes habitat destruction (see details in Chapter 3). The decision is controversial in that this provision essentially gives the federal government land-use authority over private lands.

LEGISLATIVE APPROACHES

In the 104th Congress, bills were introduced that would essentially overturn the *Sweet Home* decision by limiting the definition of "harm" to direct actions against a species that kill or injure individual members of the species.[40] Most environmental groups strongly oppose this provision, which they believe would strip the ESA of its ability to prevent habitat destruction—the primary cause of endangerment. They favor approaches that would codify or expand on the FWS's rules on the definition of "harm" to protect habitat.

One bill proposed an additional change to the Section 9 enforcement provisions by allowing the secretary to issue general permits on a county, state, regional, or nationwide basis that would exempt specific categories of activities from take liability for a period of five years.[41] This is similar to the nationwide general permit program for wetland development currently employed in the Clean Water Act. Permits would be approved only for activities that have minimal individual and cumulative adverse effects on the species. This idea, if implemented carefully, may have merit. The FWS is exploring a similar concept through the promulgation of statewide habitat conservation plans.

Critical Habitat

THE ISSUE

The designation of "critical habitat"—lands deemed essential to the survival of a species—can limit federal actions within the affected area. Such designations have become controversial of late because of concerns that they could result in restrictions on private lands as well. Prior to the 1994 elections, efforts to preserve the golden-cheeked warbler led to a public outcry when news reports suggested the FWS was planning to designate millions of acres in thirty-three Texas counties as critical habitat for the endangered bird.[42] Fearing land-use restrictions, landowners and politicians seized on the issue. Senator Kay Bailey Hutchison (R-Tex.) drafted language barring new designations of threatened or endangered species and critical habitat nationwide. It passed in 1995 as a rider to a Defense Department supplemental appropriations bill and remained in effect for one year.[43]

The FWS maintains the panic was unjustified, and the subsequent moratorium created significant delays in the listing process for other species. According to agency sources, less than 800,000 acres of potential warbler habitat even exist, much of which would not be designated critical. To date, the FWS has never formally proposed critical habitat for the bird.

The role of critical habitat is often misunderstood. It only affects federal agencies that propose to fund, authorize, or carry out activities that may have an adverse effect on listed species in the area. Federal agencies, under Section 7 of the ESA, must consult with the FWS before undertaking any activities that affect critical habitat. Although critical habitat may be designated on state or private lands, activities in those areas are not reviewed under the ESA unless there is some federal involvement. Designation of critical habitat can be an important educational and planning tool that alerts federal, state, and local interests that an area is important to endangered species. Technically, the designation could increase the chance that future regulations may affect property within the denoted area; however, the designation itself imposes no land-use restrictions whatsoever on private lands.

LEGISLATIVE APPROACHES

Proposals for addressing critical habitat concerns, both real and perceived, range from eliminating the designation to spelling out clearly the agency's responsibility to landowners when habitat is selected. Some lawmakers have tried to stipulate that critical habitat can only be designated on private land with the owner's consent and with payment of compensation. Habitat would be designated during the conservation planning process, not at the time of listing. One bill proposed a system of National Biological Diversity Reserve lands, drawn mainly from existing federal lands.[44] The bulk of critical habitat would be required to be drawn from these designated lands.

A more moderate approach responded to concerns about critical habitat by linking habitat designation with the development of a recovery plan for the species. Economic factors, which are currently considered in the drafting of critical habitat, would be considered during recovery planning. To provide some certainty for private landowners prior to development of a recovery plan, Representative Wayne Gilchrest (R-Md.) proposed requiring the secretary to publish in the *Federal Register* and local newspapers a list of those specific acts that would be included under the take prohibitions for that species.[45]

Other approaches would require designation of critical habitat with the establishment of a conservation or recovery plan to allow more time for data collection prior to designation. One bill attempted to limit critical habitat designations to areas that were occupied by the species at the time of listing and that are deemed essential to the persistence of the species over a fifty-year period. Other ideas included providing incentives for critical habitat protection through the issuance of habitat reserve grants administered by the Interior Department.

State Involvement

THE ISSUE

Many stakeholders agree that state and local governments need to play a larger role in implementing the ESA, and their assistance in recovering species is critical. A recent report of the Western Governors' Association spells out a number of ways to increase state involvement in species conservation.[46] The governors believe states with species protection programs approved by the secretary of the interior should have the option to assume the primary role in implementing certain aspects of the ESA, so long as the goals of the act are met. State assumption of wetlands programs under Section 404 of the Clean Water Act provides one precedent for this action, though it should be noted that few states have developed approved plans to implement wetlands programs.

The governors also call for increased collaboration and partnerships between states and the federal government in rule making and implementation. Incidental take permitting, in areas where HCPs are in effect, could also be delegated to the states.

LEGISLATIVE APPROACHES

Many lawmakers appear eager to increase the role of the states in endangered species protection. Some would require the secretary to consult in varying degrees with affected state and local governments on listing decisions and conservation planning.[47] Although the notion of increased state involvement is widely supported, some have proposed giving state governors the final say on listing decisions in their states. This would be a serious blow to the authority of the Interior Department in managing the ESA and could lead to disparate enforcement of the act from state to state. More moderate proposals would encourage state and local governments to enter into cooperative management agreements with the secretary to protect species or a group of species.[48]

Protection for Subspecies

THE ISSUE

Critics of the ESA argue that protection should not be provided for "subspecies," or distinct populations of species, that may be rare in one region but remain abundant elsewhere. Environmentalists maintain that that would eliminate protection for such high-profile species as the bald eagle, gray wolf, and grizzly bear. The National Research Council recently endorsed the protection of distinct population segments to maintain maximum genetic diversity.[49]

LEGISLATIVE APPROACHES

Since the publication of the NRC's report, efforts in Congress to eliminate protection for subspecies have lost ground. In the 104th Congress, most bills introduced did not change current Section 9 protections for subspecies and distinct populations. Still, some limitations have been proposed. In one bill, for example, prohibitions on the take of such species would be automatic, but to implement additional protection efforts for distinct populations the secretary would have to make a specific finding that the recommended actions were in the national interest.[50] Another bill would have provided for continued protection for subspecies and distinct populations if they can be shown to be genetically isolated.[51]

Recovery Planning

THE ISSUE

The ESA requires that all possible efforts be undertaken to "recover" species from the brink of extinction. Critics argue that this requirement is unrealistic, and it may not be possible to save all species. Some maintain that we should not even try, and that a "triage" system would permit a more reasonable allocation of scarce resources. While putting all species into the listing "ark" may be scientifically sound and perhaps ethically preferable, it may eventually weaken public support for the ESA.[52] Granted, the "charismatic megafauna" are likely to get more attention and resources, but it is debatable whether the law itself should be changed to acknowledge explicitly such political choices.

LEGISLATIVE APPROACHES

The recovery planning process is one area that is sure to be scrutinized in the reauthorization debate. Three bills propose eliminating the ESA's goal of species recovery in favor of a "conservation objective" to be established by the secretary of the interior.[53] Allowing for some variation in language, each adopted a similar approach: in preparing a recovery plan, the administration would be free to choose among a range of options from full recovery to a mere prohibition on direct take of the species. Once the objective is selected, the secretary would develop a conservation plan and must assess the economic and social impacts of the proposed alternatives. The secretary would also be required to hold at least two public hearings in the affected region. Other approaches would maintain the goal of recovery for all species and instead require the agency to prioritize actions that will have the greatest potential to recover the species. Some bills would set deadlines to speed up the recovery planning process to address both landowners' and species' needs.

Private Property Rights

THE ISSUE

Landowners are increasingly claiming that federal regulations under the ESA cause them considerable financial hardship. Relieving that burden, either through incentives or direct payments to landowners, is a priority of most reform proposals. A number of lawmakers, seeking a way to protect private property values, have proposed takings compensation measures that would require the government to pay landowners whenever regulations or federal actions diminish the value of any or all portions of a property. This approach would considerably broaden the scope of Fifth Amendment takings law, which the courts have traditionally held to require compensation only if a landowner loses all economic interest in his or her property.[54] Compensating "partial" or "regulatory" takings raises a number of serious questions, including the difficulty of establishing a reliable threshold for compensation and a process for assessing when that threshold has been breached.[55] Critics maintain a statutory compensation schedule would spawn an endless stream of litigation and bureaucratic involvement.

Property values can, of course, be positively affected by government actions. The building of a highway, construction of schools and parks, and maintenance of water and sewer systems all affect the value of property. Thompson argues that agricultural subsidies, for example, have increased the value of farmland by $250 billion. Similarly, he estimates that the income tax deduction for home mortgages boosts residential property values by $730 billion nationwide.[56] Some argue that these so-called givings should also be considered and weighed against any compensation for negative actions.

LEGISLATIVE APPROACHES

Proposed ESA reauthorization bills have addressed the need to protect private property interests, but their approaches have tended to vary dramatically. One House bill introduced in the 104th Congress provided for direct compensation to landowners who have suffered losses of more than 20 percent of their property value due to ESA requirements.[57] If the property value is diminished by 50 percent or more, landowners could require the agency to purchase the property.

Environmental organizations and the Clinton administration vehemently oppose compensation schemes, and it appears that providing direct

financial compensation to affected landowners will remain highly controversial in Congress as well. Most reauthorization bills have not included
a takings compensation provision. Some, however, have attempted to
establish as a matter of policy that the ESA should not deny individuals
the right to use their property, nor should administrative decisions reduce property values substantially. Congress may be expected to codify a
Clinton administration program exempting residential properties from
the ESA. That directive also gave the secretary the authority to exempt five
acres or less of contiguous property from the provisions of the ESA if the
proposed development does not imminently threaten the existence of
species.

Endangered species protection also could be affected by congressional
approval of property rights legislation outside the context of the ESA
reauthorization. Freestanding property rights protection bills have been
introduced in each of the most recent Congresses. Although a sweeping
compensation bill cleared the House in 1995, the full Senate has never
taken up the issue.[58] Many observers believe that property rights advocates will find less support for their cause in the 105th Congress. At this
writing, no omnibus property rights compensation bills have been introduced in this session of Congress.

Incentives Programs

THE ISSUE

A growing number of stakeholders agree that incentive programs offer
the best hope for achieving conservation goals on private lands. Collaborative programs that invite local participation are most likely to win
support and have a positive effect on species protection efforts. A variety
of incentive- and market-based approaches to species conservation are
discussed at length in the next section. Some of these are included in
proposed legislation.

LEGISLATIVE APPROACHES

Incentives represent the common ground for ESA reform legislation. Virtually every bill proposed over the past few years has attempted to provide
at least a few incentives for species conservation on private land. Many
proposals encourage early collaboration among stakeholders for private
conservation initiatives with federal assistance. In one plan, for example,
after a species is listed and a conservation objective is chosen, the interior

secretary would be required to seek out voluntary partnerships with individuals and with local and state governments through cooperative management agreements or habitat conservation plans.[59] Only after that could the department develop a federal conservation plan.

Another bill would have required the secretary to work cooperatively with private landowners and minimize economic impacts of conservation activities.[60] It also established a system prioritizing actions to protect species based on land ownership. Efforts should target federal lands first, then state and local lands. Next the agency would be required to ensure that federally subsidized activities be consistent with recovery plans. Only after pursuing economic incentive solutions could the government directly regulate activities on private lands. Other ideas included establishing a Community Assistance Program in each field office of the FWS to answer questions and assist local governments in developing habitat conservation plans and codifying the safe harbors program.[61]

Estate tax relief has been proposed for lands under conservation agreements, as have the safe harbors and "no surprises" policies developed administratively by the Interior Department.[62] A number of proposals would have increased technical assistance to landowners, and would either establish a new Conservation Reserve Program for wildlife habitat or would expand the existing Farm Bill program to enroll wildlife habitat. One bill would have provided an enhanced tax deduction for the donation of land to a conservation easement or for conservation purposes.[63]

Another bill proposed the establishment of a Theodore Roosevelt Commemorative Coin Act, which would call for the minting of commemorative coins to raise money for a new Endangered Species Habitat Trust Fund.[64] The fund would be used for habitat acquisition, easements, grants, and compensation to property owners. The authors expect the coins to generate $50 million over two years. A similar program, a commemorative coin established by Congress in 1995 to raise funds to protect Civil War battlefields, yielded just $5 million of the $21 million it had been projected to raise.

INCENTIVE PROGRAMS FOR SPECIES CONSERVATION

No strategy to preserve the nation's overall biodiversity can hope to succeed without the willing participation of private landowners. Most species routinely cross political and ownership boundaries, and 37 percent of threatened and endangered species are found only on private lands.[65] While a regulatory component is critical to species protection, much more may ultimately be achieved for wildlife and for conservation through the use of voluntary, proactive measures. A growing body of literature is emerging concerning the use of economic incentives to achieve environmental aims. As we have seen, current legislative approaches are beginning to incorporate market incentives among their provisions. Such efforts are laudable, but the range of innovative ideas available to policymakers is far greater than current bills employ. While some of these ideas may need further analysis, the work that has already been done by such groups as the Keystone Center and Defenders of Wildlife provides a useful starting point for a discussion of incentive-based policies.[66] Such dialogues suggest incentives that offer the best hope for finding common ground in this fractious debate.

A number of characteristics have been identified on which an incentive program could be based. Specifically, such programs should be voluntary, financially feasible for all participants, have a positive ecological impact, embrace partnerships, provide certainty for landowners, be implemented at the management level most suited to achieve its aims, and balance the goals of consistency and flexibility.[67]

Many incentive proposals center on changes to the federal tax code. Tax policies affect behavior in a variety of ways; therefore, it is logical to assume that shifts in tax liability to encourage conservation are both feasible and promising. Examples include income tax credits or deductions for conservation expenses, and property tax credits for lands under permanent conservation easements.

Proposals Affecting Developers

Other credit-based systems, some more theoretical than applied, could have a significant impact on species conservation. Various proposals for tradable development rights (TDRs, details of which will be spelled out below), perhaps based on the pollution trading system in the Clean Air Act Amendments of 1990, could allow for preservation of ecologically significant lands while permitting development to occur in other areas. Such a proposal would establish a market for development rights and foster a greater appreciation for the use and value of land, with consequential benefits for local and regional planning.[68]

Proposals Affecting Agricultural Lands

Voluntary incentive programs, such as Partners for Wildlife and the North American Wetlands Conservation Plan, could also be expanded with great benefits for landowners and wildlife. Administered by the Department of Agriculture under the Farm Bill program, the Conservation Reserve Program[69] and the Wetlands Reserve Program[70] have had a positive effect in restoring native vegetation complexes and increasing migratory bird populations. These programs allow landowners to enroll acres of highly erodible cropland and wetlands into a restoration program under temporary or permanent easements in exchange for cash payments. Participation is strictly voluntary. The CRP has enrolled more than 36 million acres in ten-year easements. The Wetlands Reserve Program has enrolled 250,000 acres under permanent easements.

Ironically, neither program was designed with species conservation in mind, but both have become critically important for preserving wildlife habitat. With minor statutory adjustments, they could provide even greater benefits for threatened wildlife by allowing landowners to enroll acreage on the basis of its habitat values.

A variety of federal programs already offer financial assistance to landowners to implement certain management activities on their land. Direct cash payments can be offered, as in the Conservation Reserve Program, or other forms of financial support—as in the Forest Service's Stewardship Incentive Program, Forestry Incentive Program, and Agricultural Conservation Program—can be employed. There is a long and successful precedent for these kinds of assistance programs.[71] The high number of applicants for programs like the Conservation Reserve Program attests to their popularity with landowners. These USDA conservation programs should be examined as model landowner partnerships that could be revised to ensure that species or ecosystem protection are targeted purposes.

Congress could establish an additional reserve program under the ESA that would specifically target wildlife habitat. The program could be set up very much like CRP or WRP, but it would be run by the Interior Department. Additional revolving funds could be established to encourage landowner participation in habitat conservation planning, natural communities conservation planning, or other regional approaches.[72]

The Role of Private Organizations

Private organizations can offer incentives and awards programs on their own that encourage landowners to embrace conservation. An early example is the Wolf Compensation Fund established in 1987 by Defenders of Wildlife to compensate ranchers for cattle losses incurred as a result of wolf predation. Initially viewed with skepticism by the livestock community, the program has, since its inception, paid out more than $20,000 to ranchers who have documented wolf claims. Originally targeted for Montana, into which wolves had begun migrating from Canada, the program has been expanded to cover the Yellowstone National Park and central Idaho regions in which the FWS began reintroducing gray wolves in 1995. The program also pays landowners $5,000 per den for permitting wolves that den on private property to remain there. A number of landowners are working willingly with the FWS and Defenders in cases in which wolves now reside on their property.

Other organizations have been working collaboratively with diverse interests on the local level. Groups like Ducks Unlimited, The Conservation Fund, Trout Unlimited, the Rocky Mountain Elk Foundation, American Farmland Trust, The Nature Conservancy, Trust for Public Land, Wildlife Habitat Council, and the hundreds of area land trusts are finding nongovernmental, cost-effective ways to save millions of acres of land in partnership with local people.

Estate Tax Relief

The burden of federal estate taxes often forces landowners with open space and wildlife habitat, such as farmers, ranchers, or woodland owners, who are "land rich and cash poor," to harvest resources or subdivide their property for development in order to pay the tax.[73] Estate taxes are imposed when a decedent's property value exceeds $600,000. The rate begins at 37 percent and can go as high as 55 percent for estates valued at more than $3 million. Furthermore, land is generally appraised at its "highest and best use," which, economically speaking, is most often its development potential. Changing the law to allow valuation based on current use would better reflect the ecological value and benefits of other uses.[74]

Landowners frequently identify the estate tax as a significant concern, and the environmental effects of the tax are increasingly recognized. The Northern Forest Lands Council's recent report on managing private forest resources in the Northeast called for estate tax reform as a key component of forest preservation efforts in the region.[75] This proposal would permit land to stay in family hands without significant tax liability, provided that the land was being managed under a conservation agreement. Under an estate tax deferral plan, should the heirs decide to withdraw from the conservation agreement or dispose of the property without assuring compliance of the buyer with regard to the agreement, then they would be responsible for paying the tax. Heirs can thus defer taxes for as long as they wish or escape the tax altogether by continuing to honor the conservation agreement.[76]

The goal of any estate tax reform should be to keep large tracts of species habitat intact and managed for the maximum benefit of species.

Tax Deductions for Conservation Expenses

Currently, the tax code discourages long-term management of woodlots by prohibiting nonindustrial landowners from deducting forest management expenses until the wood is harvested. Allowing landowners to deduct conservation expenses in the same year they are incurred would encourage conservation planning.[77] Another proposal would establish an Endangered Species Habitat Tax Credit, which would work like the existing Reforestation Tax Credit, to make conservation activities more cost-effective for landowners.[78]

Land Exchanges

The vast federal estate—lands managed by the Department of the Interior, the Department of Agriculture, and the Department of Defense—includes many lands that provide important habitat for wildlife. The value of these lands as endangered species habitat varies, of course, as does the commercial value of the timber, minerals, or agricultural activities on a given property. Likewise, private lands offer a variety of economic and ecological values. Where these values pose irreconcilable conflicts, opportunities may exist to adjust ownership patterns to enhance endangered species recovery and permit reasonable economic development.

Keystone proposes a multiagency Federal Land Resource and Assessment Team to identify federal lands that have limited ecological significance but may have commodity or real estate values. These lands could then be exchanged on a voluntary basis with landowners.[79] Such a program should encourage local exchanges; major shifts in land asset patterns may not be a desirable outcome and would need to be examined. Opportunities for exchanges may be limited but in individual instances could prove beneficial to all parties.

Establishment of an Endangered Species Habitat Trust Fund could complement the current Department of the Interior land exchange system. Once lands are identified for exchange, a Habitat Trust, with nonprofit corporation status under the authority of the interior secretary, could bring market forces to bear on land exchanges and help to maximize the return on the disposition of surplus lands that lack appreciable habitat value.[80]

Conservation Banking and Development Rights

Tax incentives are important and demonstrable methods of encouraging behavior on private lands that furthers conservation goals. In this tight fiscal climate, lawmakers will be increasingly pressed to find programs that are revenue neutral or impose little cost to the federal treasury. A number of the above suggestions could meet that test, but there is another class of incentives based on market principles that do not directly affect the revenue stream and deserve further consideration.

Such market-based approaches are designed to assign economic value to environmental concerns, thereby ensuring a more thoughtful weighing of costs and benefits in personal economic decisions. They also are notable in that they avoid the perception that landowners must be paid to do the right thing on their property—one of the major concerns with the various takings compensation schemes.

A system of tradable development rights, for example, would protect private property while enabling communities to manage growth and preserve ecologically significant lands. The Supreme Court has famously referred to property rights as a "bundle of sticks."[81] The system allocates development rights to landowners whose property lies in conservation zones. Such rights could be traded or sold to permit higher-than-normal development densities in other zones. Developers benefit from the certainty and predictability that designated conservation and development zones afford, and planning can proceed accordingly. TDRs can be employed to address a variety of social goals, from species protection to urban sprawl to affordable housing.

One community where TDR systems are being employed is the New Jersey Pinelands, a 1.1-million-acre area of pine and oak forests, rivers and streams, and towns in southern New Jersey. The region includes the Cohansey Aquifer and habitat for 580 native plant species (including 54 threatened or endangered species), 299 bird species, 91 fish, 59 reptiles, and 39 mammals—all sandwiched between such major metropolitan areas as New York City and Philadelphia.[82]

A similar program, the Habitat Transaction Method, is an innovative approach currently being developed for the Kern County, California, Habitat Conservation Plan. Like TDR, this method would enable communities to undertake advanced planning through the use of development rights. HTM is different in that it assigns a particular value to a property based on scientific assessments of its habitat. Development would not be prohibited anywhere, but varying levels of mitigation would be required according to the quality of habitat being affected. Developers wishing to impact habitat in the "red zone," the highest-valued area, would be required to create, say, nine conservation credits per acre, while development in less sensitive areas might require only three mitigation credits to proceed. HTMs afford greater flexibility for communities and avoid the possible controversy that encouraging higher-than-normal-density development might breed in a given neighborhood. While there is no guarantee in this system that the most valuable lands will be preserved, some safeguards are built in, and if coupled with a land acquisition mechanism, that concern could be addressed easily.[83] In the short run, mitigation banking is expected to play a greater role than habitat transaction models in the region.

Zoning is primarily a local issue, and state and county governments are increasingly turning to such tools as transferable development rights, real estate transfer taxes, exaction fees, and other programs to achieve growth-management objectives. The federal role in such issues may by nature be limited, but technical assistance and guidelines, such as the federal standards for wetland mitigation banking, could be employed on a local or regional basis. Federal incentive grants to participating states might also be available.

Conservation banking is another idea that is gaining credence as a tool for species protection. The Bank of America, in partnership with the California Resource Agency, for example, recently established a conservation habitat bank for gnatcatcher habitat in Southern California. Under this plan, a public or private entity acquires land deemed valuable for habitat conservation and manages the land to enhance those values. These lands are then used to mitigate the impacts of future development in the region. In the context of a regional plan, mitigation banking can have broad conservation benefits while increasing the economic value of preserved habitat.[84] In addition, the Gatlin Development Co. is putting together an 1,800-acre mitigation bank near El Cajon that could expand to 2,400 acres. The most unusual players in the mitigation bank are the Boys and Girls Clubs of San Diego, which are raising money by creating a 300-acre mitigation bank from donated land that could grow to 1,100 acres.

Market mechanisms and economic incentives are innovative and potentially beneficial conservation tools. Such strategies, however, would best supplement, rather than supplant, the existing regulatory framework. As Clark and Downes[85] note, "Regulatory standards . . . are vitally important for defining the context within which important market mechanisms operate, and to provide a baseline of protection in situations where market incentives are not strong enough to provide environmental protection." Market-based incentives have the advantage of increasing flexibility for planners or developers of habitat conservation plans while recognizing private sector initiatives. Such opportunities should be fully explored.

OTHER MODEL PROGRAMS

The North American Plans

In an attempt to protect biodiversity and build positive relations with private property owners, it is important to look beyond the ESA and examine other models that are proving successful. To counter two hundred years of wetland degradation and related declines in waterfowl populations throughout the North American continent, a most ambitious cooperative habitat conservation effort was launched during the Reagan administration and given a major boost during the Bush administration.

Signed in 1986, the North American Waterfowl Management Plan establishes public and private partnerships to reverse waterfowl declines by conserving, restoring, and enhancing wetland habitat. Scientists estimate that fewer than 100 million acres of wetlands remain across the country out of an estimated 220 million acres that existed two hundred years ago.[86] Since three-quarters of the nation's remaining wetlands are on private lands, the success of the NAWMP clearly depends on nonregulatory and completely voluntary mechanisms adopted by property owners. Its international mission is fourfold: (1) recover waterfowl to levels observed in the 1970s by the year 2001 by restoring wetlands and associated upland habitat; (2) conserve biological diversity; (3) integrate conservation with sustainable economic development; and (4) promote partnerships between federal and state government, nonprofits, and the private sector.[87] The plan implemented a first-of-its-kind system of partnerships called "joint ventures" to carry out long-term habitat restoration.

Passed by the 101st Congress and signed into law by President Bush on 13 December 1989, the related North American Wetlands Conservation Act provided substantial funding through a new matching grants program to encourage these partnerships and provide resources for cooperative work at the site or wetland. As of March 1996, $164.7 million in NAWCA funds has been expended, an average of about $24 million per year over the seven years.[88]

The results have been overwhelming. During the ten years since the initiation of the NAWMP, some 3 million acres of habitat have been preserved or restored through more than two thousand partnerships using about $700 million in sponsor contributions.[89] In addition, over 20 million acres of wetlands in Mexico have benefited from the North American Plan through enhancement, management reserves, and education. Land conservation expenditures in the United States have averaged only about $230 per acre.[90] The focus of the North American initiative has been wetlands and waterfowl, but the program has reaped substantial benefits for nongame fish and wildlife, including endangered species. Waterfowl are superb indicators of the biological integrity of certain productive ecosystems. Wetlands include swamps, bogs, marshes, riparian habitats along streams and rivers, and coastal estuaries, but these cover only 5 percent of the landscape of the lower forty-eight states. Even so, it is estimated that up to one-third of threatened plants and two-thirds of endangered animals are wetlands dependent. More than 40 percent of all listed threatened and endangered species use wetlands sometime during their life cycles.[91]

The North American Plan's approach is a successful model for forming voluntary partnerships to enact positive change across the landscape to conserve and enhance living resources. It draws upon the land ethic many property owners share and targets their efforts to protect one of the nation's most important and diverse habitats. All species benefit from the effort.

CASE STUDIES: NORTH AMERICAN PLANS

Ace Basin, South Carolina. In the 22,000-acre Cheehaw-Combahee Reserve of the ACE Basin complex, private landowners joined the Army Corps of Engineers, the FWS, the South Carolina Wildlife and Marine Resource Department, and nonprofits to implement a 3,200-acre water-impoundment system and estuarine wetland habitat restoration to benefit such listed species as the American alligator, shortnose sturgeon, southern bald eagle, and wood stork.[92]

Mad Island Marsh, Texas. Dow Chemical, Ducks Unlimited, The Nature Conservancy, and other nonprofit organizations joined landowners and state and federal agencies in a 5,800-acre effort to protect freshwater wetlands and upland coastal prairie and enhance rice fields to benefit five federally listed, five federal-candidate, and one state-threatened species, including the peregrine falcon, brown pelican, piping plover, reddish egret, Texas horned lizard, white-tailed hawk, and the long-billed curlew.[93]

Llano Seco Ranch, California. With a large livestock operation, Llano Seco Ranch represented the largest unprotected block of riparian forest and wetlands remaining in the Sacramento Valley. Ranch owners entered into a cooperative plan with FWS, California's Department of Fish and Game, and several nonprofit groups in 1991 to conserve and restore 14,000 acres of wetland and riparian habitat, native grasslands, and oak savannas. Improved livestock management practices were voluntarily adopted to benefit a host of wildlife species that were listed or of special concern under state and federal laws. Wintering bald eagles, peregrine falcons, Swainson's hawks, and tricolor blackbirds have used the wetland habitat. The valley's elderberry longhorn beetle and the state's last remaining spring run of Chinook salmon are dependent on the ranch's riparian habitat.[94]

Central Valley, California. California had suffered a 91 percent reduction in wetlands by the mid-1980s, and more than 90 percent of the Central Valley's once vast expanse of riparian forests, oak woodlands, emergent wetland, and native grasslands have been converted or severely degraded by agriculture and urban development.[95] Yet the Central Valley, supporting 60 percent of the total Pacific Flyway population, is essential as a wintering area for migratory waterfowl. During the past eight years under the North American Plan and the Wetlands Conservation Act, the Central Valley Habitat Joint Venture has been successful in protecting over 67,000 acres of wetlands and restoring over 34,000 acres.

Partners for Wildlife

As landowners face complex choices on how best to manage their property, a growing number are voluntarily incorporating wildlife habitat restoration techniques into their management strategies with the help of outside partners and are realizing the associated benefits. In 1987, the FWS initiated a program to rehabilitate wetlands. The program was broadened and renamed Partners for Wildlife by the Bush administration. With a budget of $10 million in FY 1995, the Partners program now offers technical assistance and some restoration funding to willing landowners. More than one-third of the total nationwide cost of the program has come from other participants such as the U.S. Department of Agriculture, state wildlife agencies, and groups like the National Fish and Wildlife Foundation, Ducks Unlimited, and the Audubon Society.[96]

This modest program has achieved impressive results—13,000 ranchers, farmers, and other property owners have willingly joined Partners to restore over 300,000 acres of previously degraded wetlands and 30,000 acres of native uplands and prairies. In addition, 350 miles of riparian habitat and 40 miles of in-stream habitat have been rehabilitated.[97] Since the program focuses on some of the more productive inland habitat types, benefits are provided to a broad complex of federal trust species— migratory birds, fisheries, and at-risk resources. Although listed species have not been specifically targeted by Partners, approximately 15 percent of projects implemented around the nation in 1995 improved habitat for listed and candidate species. In western regions of the country, a majority of the 1995 projects benefited such species.[98] Project costs range from $104 per acre in the Southeast to $40 per acre in the Intermountain West.[99]

Ironically, although Partners is recognized as one of the most successful private property programs administered by a federal agency, Secretary Bruce Babbitt at one time urged its termination as a part of his reinventing government efforts. More recently, a safe harbor policy was adopted for Partners to encourage even greater participation in the program. Landowners who agree to undertake cooperative habitat conservation agreements to restore habitat can later choose to return their lands to pre-restoration conditions even if listed species become established on their property.

CASE STUDIES: PARTNERS FOR WILDLIFE

Oklahoma. The Oklahoma Private Lands initiative has been an ambitious cooperative involving landowners, the National Fish and Wildlife Foundation, and the Oklahoma Ecological Services Office of FWS with such partners as the Oklahoma Department of Wildlife Conservation, The Nature Conservancy, and the George M. Sutton Avian Research Center. OPL has focused on educational outreach and habitat restoration. To date, three hundred landowners have joined in the enhancement and protection of more than 10,000 acres. Nearly 500,000 citizens, the majority of them youngsters, have been exposed to the value of wetlands through the "Wetlands = Wonderlands" program. Tourism professionals have been contacted to demonstrate the monetary value of marketing the state's wildlife. Wildlife-specific events and exhibits attracting thousands of participants have been conducted.[100]

Virginia. The cooperation of landowners is the key to restoring a diverse aquatic complex of at-risk species in the Upper Tennessee River Basin in southwest Virginia. Nearly 90 percent of the Clinch and Powell River watershed region is in private ownership. Voluntary activities for riparian-zone protection included fencing livestock, bank stabilization, and replantings to buffer streams from runoff from surrounding agricultural areas. The Basin contains twenty-six listed species, including fourteen endangered freshwater mussels (one of North America's most imperiled fauna groups) and six fish species.[101]

California. In partnership with a landowner, the Casa de Patos project took 450 acres of leveled rice fields and recontoured them to natural topography, hydrology, and vegetation. Tens of thousands of ducks, geese, swans, shorebirds, and cranes now use the habitat, while the threatened giant garter snake (*Thamnophis gigas*) and state-listed species of concern like the Swainson's hawk (*Buteo swainsoni*) have also benefited.[102]

Kansas. The state's only outcropping of the Ozarkian Plateau and its unique cave system will be protected and restored by willing landowners who have agreed to restrict vehicular access. The endangered gray bat (*Myotis grisescens*), along with four state-listed species, three mammals, two amphibians, a neotropical migratory bird, and forty-three other plan species will benefit from the project.[103]

Arizona. At Cottonwood Spring, a landowner has agreed to restore a declining cottonwood-willow riparian corridor and wetland with exclusion fencing and the installation of a solar-powered water pump to supply his livestock. Return of vegetative components of the sensitive spring and wetland corridor are benefiting the endangered Gila top minnow; a listed species, the Huachuca water umbel; and the listed southwestern willow flycatcher.[104]

Wyoming. Near Centennial in the southern part of the state, landowners have cooperated in the restoration of wetlands on their property to return the historic habitat for the endangered Wyoming toad (*Bufo hemiophrys baxteri*) and the boreal toad (*Bufo boreas boreas*).[105]

Michigan. Habitat is being restored for the endangered Kirtland's warbler (*Dendroica kirtlandii*) by returning three hundred acres of private lands to younger, successional jack pine forests. Several other species, including the Nashville warbler, chickadee, brown thrasher, rufous-sided towhee, and the hermit thrush, will also benefit from this Partner's cooperative project.[106]

Partners in Flight

Launched in 1990 by the Bush administration in partnership with the National Fish and Wildlife Foundation and other public/private allies, Partners in Flight is a consortium of hundreds of private business, landowner, industry association, nonprofit organization, and natural resource agency partners dedicated to nonregulatory and cooperative efforts to maintain healthy avian populations in the United States and across the Western Hemisphere.[107] The effort was prompted by the alarming decline in neotropical migrant birds in the Atlantic states and Midwest grassland and West Coast regions of the country.

With a primary motto of "Keeping Common Birds Common," the program focuses on wildlife resources that are growing in popularity with millions of Americans and also producing millions of dollars for local communities in nonconsumptive activities such as photography and bird-watching. Partners in Flight is based on the idea that the most economically and scientifically efficient approach to avian conservation is to take actions to keep species from becoming rare or endangered. Some of the program projects, however, do involve already-listed species.

During its seven years of operation, more than one thousand different projects have been undertaken, ranging from habitat restoration and regional monitoring to environmental outreach to public school education. A California Riparian Habitat Joint Venture has been established by citizen groups, landowners, and governmental agencies to initiate research and educational efforts and also to rehabilitate thousands of acres of riparian woodlots to benefit avian diversity, encouraging such species as the endangered least Bell's vireo (*Vireo bellii pusillus*) and the Southwest willow flycatcher (*Empidonax trailii*). Under Partners in Flight agreements, fourteen timber companies, including Champion, International Paper, and Hancock, are making strong commitments to develop mechanisms to protect the endangered red-cockaded woodpeckers inhabiting longleaf pine forests on their private lands while also maintaining the production of timber and its related jobs in the Southeast. Landowners in Texas have agreed to the promotion of habitat-enhancement and stewardship practices to benefit a variety of migratory birds including the endangered black-capped vireo (*Vireo atricapillus*) and golden-cheeked warbler.[108]

Supplementary to the Partners in Flight program, the Western Governors' Association initiated the Great Plains Project in 1992 under the leadership of Wyoming's Governor Mike Sullivan (D-Wyo.); Mike Hayden, the former Department of the Interior assistant secretary for Parks & Wildlife and former governor of Kansas; and coauthor John F. Turner. This is a proactive, multistate approach by the Intermountain West states to research and implement habitat conservation of declining nongame species in order to prevent them from becoming endangered.

Teaming with Wildlife

Polls indicate that the vast majority of Americans support wildlife conservation as a core value. The last national survey, in 1991, of wildlife-dependent recreation revealed that 77 million people spend part of their time in wildlife-related pursuits. In the process, these enthusiasts spent about $100 billion per year on wildlife-related activities.[109]

Under the public trust doctrine, states have jurisdiction over most wildlife species. The federal government only has jurisdiction over such groups as migratory birds, anadromous fisheries, and species listed under the ESA. Yet for decades, most states have had a self-imposed "unfunded mandate" to conserve and manage *all* fish and wildlife resources. Although states have been responsible for hundreds of wildlife types, professional management and scientific resources have been targeted mostly

at three major groups: (1) game animals, (2) predators and pests—
"varmints" with a negative impact on specific economic activities—and
(3) threatened and endangered species (since 1973). In Wyoming, for example, there are 112 varieties of fish, bird, and mammal "game" species
out of a total species count of 634 fish, bird, mammal, reptile, and am-
phibian types.[110]

More attention to the multitude of species outside of these three traditional categories would do much to stem declines in the nation's biodiversity. Most state wildlife agencies do the best they can in conserving
multispecies systems, but resources are limited throughout the country.
For many years, the consumptive user, or sportsman, has paid for most of
the funding for wildlife conservation. In 1991, license-fee revenues from
hunters and anglers amounted to $898 million and provided the back-
bone for state wildlife resource programs. In addition, sportsmen and
gun-and-tackle manufacturers agreed decades ago to a 10 percent user fee
on firearms, ammunition, fishing tackle, and certain small engine fuels.
These revenues went to two Sport Fisheries and Wildlife Restoration accounts. In 1995, these accounts provided another $411 million to states
for wildlife conservation, with much of it dedicated to habitat conservation.[111] Over $5 billion in federal use fees has been generated from the
hunting and fishing public through these two programs and matched with
state resources.

In an effort to provide additional funding for the multitude of species
that are not pursued by hunters or anglers, and are not covered under the
ESA, diverse groups have been working under the umbrella of the International Association of Fish and Wildlife Agencies to explore new approaches.[112] A new proposal, the Fish and Wildlife Diversity Funding Initiative, was outlined, broadening the concept of "user pays" beyond just
the consumptive user. Now called Teaming with Wildlife, this proposal
would call for a smaller user fee, between one-quarter of 1 percent and
5 percent, on the manufacturer's price of such equipment as binoculars,
cameras, bird feed, canoes, hiking boots, camping equipment, and other
gear used by outdoor enthusiasts who enjoy wild critters and wild places.
The actual amount to be raised would depend on the specifics of enacted
legislation, but estimates are in the $350-million-per-year range. Under
the proposed legislation, the Fish and Wildlife Conservation Enhancement Act of 1996, these new revenues would mostly be redistributed back
to the states (using the same formula as with the existing user fee accounts), and such revenues could be used for "nongame" research, edu-

cation, and management and for innovative state models of cooperative stewardship projects on private lands.[113]

CONCLUSION

In 1992, when the black-footed ferret reintroduction began, a number of landowners took a leap of faith to participate in an effort that was uncertain at best, intrusive at worst. Not everything worked perfectly; the ferret is still in danger of extinction, though its chance of survival has improved. The real success story, however, is not the number of ferrets on the ground but the change in attitudes that a flexible cooperative management approach under the ESA helped bring about.

Jack Turnell's Pitchfork Ranch was the place where the ferret was rediscovered after it had been presumed extinct. Turnell could have refused to participate in its recovery. He could have adopted the "shoot, shovel, and shut up" mentality that some have suggested to avoid dealing with the ESA. Instead, Turnell got involved with the species and, in the process, became a believer in the power and promise of collaboration. "The ferret forced me to cooperate with people who I'd traditionally been an adversary of," he says. "I realized then I could work with them and not feel threatened."[114]

This chapter has illustrated the importance of proactive, collaborative programs to achieve conservation goals. Examples abound of existing programs that are successfully saving biodiversity while making partners of America's landowners. The ESA already provides for a variety of cooperative approaches, but additional models need to be developed and incorporated into the act. Reauthorization of the ESA is an opportunity to promote partnership, explore incentives, and foster cooperation out on the land. It can be done. If we are to achieve meaningful conservation goals in this country, it must be done. Adherence to the simplistic arguments of the extremes in this debate will only impede conservation progress and further polarize the decision-making process.

In his first inaugural address, Thomas Jefferson said, "Not every difference of opinion is a difference of principle." It is important to remember that when considering how to reconcile what appear to be diametrically opposing views. The dialogues sponsored by the Keystone Center and Defenders of Wildlife involved diverse gatherings of stakeholders and showed how much common ground really exists on these issues.

Most Americans support endangered species protection and property rights, and they continue to believe that economic interests and conservation interests are compatible. Unfortunately, the debate, with its focus on conflict, promotes mistrust and division and squelches opportunities for collaboration. A more civil dialogue is essential to finding solutions to natural resource dilemmas. As Endicott[115] writes: "All involved must realize that land conservation works best when economic interests and ecological values are mutually supportive—and that both public and private sectors must work hard to ensure that this happens."

We must also recognize how times have changed. Increasingly, the roles of the public and private sectors have blurred. In a recent report on land conservation priorities, the National Research Council[116] concluded: "Public and private values cannot be conveniently separated. The vigorous pursuit of public values no longer takes place only on public lands or out-of-the-way preserves and set-asides. Just as federal lands host a broad array of private uses and ownership rights, private lands are shouldering an increasing public responsibility in the areas of conservation, environmental protection, and public interest health and recreation." Finding the proper balance of public and private responsibilities is not easy and will take time. Both sectors have an important role to play.

What is needed now is an informed discussion at the national level about the extent of the biodiversity crisis and what commitment the nation is willing to make in order to stem the tide of species and habitat loss. Adequate resources from a variety of public and private sources will be critical to any meaningful national effort. In this tight fiscal climate, it will take a strong public conviction that species preservation is important if the necessary resources are to be wrested from other programs. That may yet happen. "A nation that has paid farmers not to grow pigs may yet find the will to pay them to grow owls, eagles or hedgerows."[117] Various incentive programs should be adopted to encourage the active participation of landowners in species preservation.

Land-use decisions at the community level, more than anything else, will determine the shape and vitality of the landscape in the future. Federal and state programs can contribute a great deal to conservation, but local governments and individuals must do their part as well. The land ethic must be strengthened.

The controversy over the ESA is not merely about one statute and its effect on people. It is an age-old debate about the proper role of government, the conflict between economic and social interests, and our ethical obligations to other living things and to future generations. All of these dilemmas are manifest in discussions of the ESA and its importance. As Aldo Leopold[118] said: "We shall never achieve harmony with the land, any more than we shall achieve absolute justice or liberty for people. In these higher aspirations the important thing is not to achieve, but to strive." The limits of governmental regulation are increasingly being recognized. Regulations, while important, can only achieve so much before resistance serves to undermine the very purpose of the statute. Public-private partnerships offer the best hope for achieving conservation goals in the next century. In fashioning a new ESA—one that works better for wildlife and landowners—we should strive to develop cooperative models that reflect this new paradigm.

NOTES

1   In National Research Council, *Setting Priorities for Land Conservation* (Washington, D.C.: National Academy Press, 1993).

2   M. J. Bean, Perspective on Endangered Species and Private Lands: Presentation to the National Education and Training Center's Forum on the Endangered Species Act—Private Land Strategies for Working Together, 14 November 1996 (draft).

3   M. J. Bean, *Creating an Incentive for Endangered Species Conservation through Estate Tax Reform* (Environmental Defense Fund, 1996).

4   Ibid.

5   Ibid.

6   R. Dubos, *The Wooing of the Earth* (New York: Charles Scribner's Sons, 1980).

7   S. L. Yaffee, The Northern Spotted Owl: An Indicator of the Importance of Sociopolitical Context, in *Endangered Species Recovery: Finding the Lessons, Improving the Process,* ed. T. W. Clark, R. P. Reading, and A. L. Clarke (Washington, D.C.: Island Press, 1994).

8   Fish and Wildlife Service, personal communication, 1996.

9   FWS, Habitat Conservation Planning Efforts of the Southeast Region (Atlanta: U.S. Fish and Wildlife Service, 1996).

10   Ibid.

11   FWS, *Report to Congress: Endangered and Threatened Species Recovery Program* (Washington, D.C.: U.S. Department of the Interior, 1995), 64 pp.

12   W. K. Stevens, Salvation at Hand for a California Landscape, *New York Times,* 27 February 1996.

13   Ibid.

14   Ibid. Also see FWS and California Department of Fish and Game, Memorandum of Understanding Regarding Coastal Sage Scrub Natural Community Conservation Planning, 1991.

15   Stevens, Salvation at Hand for a California Landscape.
16   Ibid.
17   Ibid.
18   FWS, *Report to Congress: Endangered and Threatened Species Recovery Program.*
19   D. Hawkins, Safe Harbors, *Endangered Species Bulletin* 20, no. 3(1995):11.
20   FWS, *Final Habitat Conservation Plan to Encourage Voluntary Restoration and Enhancement of Habitat for Red-Cockaded Woodpeckers on Private and Certain Other Land in the Sandhills Region of North Carolina by Providing "Safe Harbor" to Participating Landowners* (Clemson, Ga.: U.S. Fish and Wildlife Service, 1995), 9 pp.
21   Hawkins, Safe Harbors.
22   See FWS, Final Environmental Assessment on Issuance of an Incidental Take Permit under Section 10(a)(1)(B) of the Endangered Species Act to Ralph Costa, 1995.
23   Hawkins, Safe Harbors.
24   Mark A. Cantrell, FWS, personal communication, 1996.
25   FWS, Red-Cockaded Woodpecker Fact Sheet: Conservation Strategies and Programs on Private Lands, 1995.
26   Janice Nicholls, FWS, personal communication, 1996.
27   FWS, *Final Habitat Conservation Plan.*
28   Department of the Interior, Fish and Wildlife Service, and Department of Commerce, National Oceanic and Atmospheric Administration, Announcement of Draft Safe Harbor Policy, *Federal Register* 62, no. 113(1997):32178–32183.
29   Department of the Interior, Fish and Wildlife Service, Safe Harbor Agreements and Candidate Conservation Agreements: Proposed Rule, *Federal Register* 62, no. 113(1997):32189–32194.
30   Department of the Interior, Fish and Wildlife Service, and Department of Commerce, National Oceanic and Atmospheric Administration, No Surprises Policy, *Federal Register* 62, no. 103(1997):29091–29098.
31   Department of the Interior, Fish and Wildlife Service and Department of Commerce, National Oceanic and Atmospheric Administration, Announcement of Draft Policy for Candidate Conservation Agreements, *Federal Register* 62, no. 113(1997):32183–32188.
32   Department of the Interior, Fish and Wildlife Service, Safe Harbor Agreements and Candidate Conservation Agreements.
33   FWS, Plum Creek, Federal and State Agencies Announce Grizzly Bear Conservation Agreement (Washington, D.C.: U.S. Fish and Wildlife Service, 1995).
34   Plum Creek, Swan Valley Grizzly Bear Conservation Agreement Fact Sheet, Plum Creek Timber Company, Issued with Press Release, Missoula, Montana, 2 March 1995, 8 pp.
35   Plum Creek, News Release, Plum Creek Timber Co., U.S. Fish and Wildlife Service, Flathead National Forest, Montana Department of Natural Resources and Conservation, Lakewood, Colo., 18 December 1995, 2 pp.
36   D. Dale, A. Purvis, T. Lockamy, and S. Thompson, Collaborative Problem-Solving in Cameron County, TX: The Coexistence Committee, draft article for *American Journal of Alternative Agriculture* (College Station: Texas A&M University, 1995).

37 See generally H.R. 2374 and H.R. 2444, 104th Congress (1995).

38 See H.R. 2275, 104th Congress (1995).

39 NRC, *Science and the Endangered Species Act* (Washington, D.C.: National Academy Press, 1995).

40 See S. 768, S. 1364, and H.R. 2275, all 104th Congress (1995).

41 See S. 768, 104th Congress (1995).

42 See J. Rylander, ESA Opponents Fight Warbler Habitat Designation, *Land Letter,* 1 September 1994, 2–3.

43 See H.R. 889, 104th Congress (1995), calling for "Emergency supplemental appropriations and recissions for the Department of Defense to preserve and enhance military readiness."

44 See H.R. 2275, 104th Congress (1995).

45 See H.R. 2374, 104th Congress (1995).

46 Western Governors' Association, Essential Elements of Amendments to the Endangered Species Act (Unpublished memorandum, 1995).

47 See S. 768, 104th Congress (1995).

48 See H.R. 2275, 104th Congress (1995).

49 NRC, *Science and the Endangered Species Act.*

50 See S. 768, 104th Congress (1995).

51 See S. 1364, 104th Congress (1995).

52 C. C. Mann and M. L. Plummer, *Noah's Choice: The Future of Endangered Species* (New York: Alfred A. Knopf, 1995).

53 See S. 768, S. 1364, and H.R. 2275, all 104th Congress (1995).

54 D. L. Callies, ed., *Takings* (Chicago: American Bar Association, 1996).

55 J. Echeverria, *Let the People Judge* (Washington, D.C.: Island Press, 1995).
    R. G. Converse, Property Rights Legislation: Some Questions, in *Takings,* ed. Callies.

56 E. Thompson, Jr., The Government Giveth, *Environmental Forum* (March/ April 1994):22–23.
    D. Clark and D. Downes, *What Price Biodiversity? Economic Incentives and Biodiversity Conservation in the United States* (Washington, D.C.: Center for International Environmental Law [CIEL], 1995).

57 See H.R. 2275, 104th Congress (1995).

58 H.R. 925, 104th Congress (1995), entitled Private Property Protection Act of 1995, passed in the House on 3 March 1995 and was referred to the Senate on 7 March 1995, whereupon no further action was taken.

59 See S. 768, 104th Congress (1995).

60 See H.R. 2374, 104th Congress (1995).

61 Ibid.

62 See S. 1364 and H.R. 2275, 104th Congress (1995).

63 Ibid.

64 Ibid.

65 General Accounting Office, Endangered Species Act: Information on Species Protection on Nonfederal Lands, GAO/RCED-95-16 (Washington, D.C., 1994).

66 The Keystone Center, *The Keystone Dialogue on Incentives for Private Landowners to Protect Endangered Species: Final Report* (Keystone, Colo., 1995).

R. M. Ferris, *Economic Incentives and Private Lands: Policy Options for the Endangered Species Act* (Washington, D.C.: Defenders of Wildlife, 1996).

67 The Keystone Center, *The Keystone Dialogue on Incentives for Private Landowners to Protect Endangered Species: Final Report.*

68 T. G. Olson, D. D. Murphy, and R. D. Thornton, Habitat Transaction Methods: A Proposal for Creating Tradable Credits in Endangered Species Habitat, in *Building Economic Incentives into the Endangered Species Act,* ed. H. Fischer and W. Hudson (Washington, D.C.: Defenders of Wildlife, 1994).

69 7 U.S.C. 1281 § 1231–1254.

70 7 U.S.C. 1421 § 1237–1437F.

71 J. H. Goldstein and H. T. Heintz Jr., *Incentives for Private Conservation of Species and Habitat: An Economic Perspective* (Washington, D.C.: Defenders of Wildlife, 1993).

72 Ferris, *Economic Incentives and Private Lands.*

73 The Keystone Center, *The Keystone Dialogue on Incentives for Private Landowners to Protect Endangered Species: Final Report.*

74 Ferris, *Economic Incentives and Private Lands.*
T. W. Clark, R. P. Reading, and A. L. Clarke, eds., *Endangered Species Recovery: Finding the Lessons, Improving the Process* (Washington, D.C.: Island Press, 1994).

75 Northern Forests Lands Council, Finding Common Ground: Conserving the Northern Forest: The Recommendations of the Northern Forest Lands Council, 1994.

76 The Keystone Center, *The Keystone Dialogue on Incentives for Private Landowners to Protect Endangered Species: Final Report.*

77 Ibid.
Ferris, *Economic Incentives and Private Lands.*
Northern Forests Lands Council, Finding Common Ground.

78 The Keystone Center, *The Keystone Dialogue on Incentives for Private Landowners to Protect Endangered Species: Final Report.*

79 Ibid.

80 Ibid.

81 See, for example, *Nollan v. California Coastal Community,* 483 U.S. 825, 831 (1987).

82 Clark and Downes, *What Price Biodiversity?*
N.J. Pinelands Commission, A Brief History of the New Jersey Pinelands and the Pinelands Comprehensive Management Plan, 1989.

83 Clark and Downes, *What Price Biodiversity?*

84 Ferris, *Economic Incentives and Private Lands.*

85 Clark and Downes, *What Price Biodiversity?*

86 T. E. Dahl, *Wetland Losses in the United States, 1780s to 1980s* (Washington, D.C.: U.S. Department of the Interior, Fish and Wildlife Service, 1990).

87 See FWS, A Summary of the North American Wetlands Conservation Act (Washington, D.C.: U.S. Fish and Wildlife Service, 1995).

88 See FWS, North American Wetlands Conservation Act Fact Sheet, 1996.

89 B. K. Williams, *The North American Waterfowl Management Plan Ten Years Later:*

Accomplishments and Prospects for the Future (Arlington, Va.: U.S. Fish and Wild-life Service, 1996).

90 Ibid.
91 Ibid.
92 Ibid.
93 Ibid.
94 Ibid.
95 Dahl, *Wetland Losses in the United States, 1780s to 1980s.*
96 FWS, *Partners for Wildlife: T&E Species Habitat Restoration on Private Lands* (Washington, D.C.: U.S. Fish and Wildlife Service, Division of Habitat Conservation, 1995), 2 pp.
97 D. MacLean, Partners for Wildlife, *Endangered Species Bulletin* 21, no. 1(1996).
98 Ibid.
99 FWS, *Partners for Wildlife: T&E Species Habitat Restoration on Private Lands.*
100 FWS, Oklahoma Private Lands Initiative: Final Report to the National Fish and Wildlife Foundation, Grant #93-131 (U.S. Fish and Wildlife Service, Oklahoma Ecological Services State Office, 1995), 68 pp.
101 FWS, *Partners for Wildlife: T&E Species Habitat Restoration on Private Lands.*
102 Ibid.
103 MacLean, Partners for Wildlife.
104 Ibid.
105 Ibid.
106 FWS, *Partners for Wildlife: T&E Species Habitat Restoration on Private Lands.*
107 D. R. Petit, Partners in Flight: Working with Landowners to Protect Endangered Species and Economic Opportunities, unpublished report (Arlington, Va.: U.S. Fish and Wildlife Service, Office of Migratory Bird Management, 1995), 2 pp.
108 Ibid.
109 FWS, *The 1996 Fishing, Hunting, and Wildlife-Associated Recreation* (Washington, D.C.: U.S. Fish and Wildlife Service, 1997).
110 Ibid.
111 Ibid.
112 Ibid.
113 Ibid.
114 D. Dagget, *Beyond the Rangeland Conflict: Toward a West That Works* (Layton, Utah: Gibbs-Smith, 1995).
115 E. Endicott, *Land Conservation through Public/Private Partnerships* (Washington, D.C.: Island Press, 1993).
116 NRC, *Setting Priorities for Land Conservation.*
117 Ibid.
118 A. Leopold, *A Sand County Almanac* (New York: Oxford University Press, 1949).

❄ 7 ❄

Principles to Measure the Endangered Species Act Reauthorization Debate

Policy Board of the Institute for Environment and Natural Resources

The University of Wyoming's Institute for Environment and Natural Resources Policy Board devoted its May 1996 forum to a discussion focusing on the ESA and private property. Prior to the forum, the Institute commissioned a research study panel of University of Wyoming faculty and external experts, who provided the board a summary and analysis of the key policy issues. The research study panel's work comprises Chapters 2–6 of this book. This forum provided a useful opportunity for people from diverse interests to express concerns and to build consensus on approaches to reasonable solutions. Based on their discussions, and drawing on Chapters 2–6, the Institute board members (listed below) recommend consideration of the following eight principles related to the ESA and private property during reauthorization discussions. The principles were established through a consensus process facilitated by the Keystone Center. They are not intended to be a comprehensive treatment of the complex issues associated with the ESA, but rather to provide a foundation for progress toward resolving private property issues.

1. Implementation of the ESA should engage local stakeholders in a variety of substantive roles.

Affected landowners should be involved in the ESA process for three reasons: (a) they have a right to know and to understand what is going on; (b) the process will work better if they understand it from the beginning and have a vested interest in the process; and (c) they may have input that improves implementation and generates support for the creation of novel solutions. Successful efforts at stakeholder involvement are based upon three interrelated components: communication, education, and co-operation. Each of these components should involve a two-way exchange between stakeholders and those responsible for regulations. Good communication and easy access to information are the first steps, as they can greatly reduce the distrust property owners feel about the process and help to maintain more objective and civil discourse.

Efforts should be made to simplify and broadly disseminate information on endangered species so that laypersons can understand the issues—both biological and economic—as well as the trade-offs to be made in creating solutions. In addition, internships or employee exchanges could be developed among corporations, small businesses, government agencies, academic institutions, and environmental organizations to promote the exchange of ideas and understanding of different viewpoints.

Good communication and education will help lead to cooperative solutions. Local involvement and broad public participation in developing solutions are necessary, but frequently neglected, components of government regulations. Numerous success stories with habitat conservation plans, conservation agreements, and safe harbor provisions demonstrate that local stakeholder involvement can lead to safe, responsible, and practical solutions while still maintaining accountability to national interests in preserving species (see Chapter 5). Reauthorization of the ESA should build on these successes by providing agencies with the authority to enter into agreements with landowners engaged in such efforts, and by actively promoting experimentation on a site-specific and/or species-specific basis. In order to facilitate good communication between landowners and the agencies, the fear of restrictions (i.e., disincentives) needs to be removed.

The process for listing threatened and endangered species is a major concern to private landowners because many people fear the financial consequences of having listed species on their land. While the listing procedure currently includes steps for informing the public, implementation of this public information process is not always effective. The board, while maintaining the listing authority provided to the agencies by the act, supports greater efforts to inform and involve stakeholders during the listing process.

2. *The ESA should provide private property owners with goal-based flexibility in the management and recovery of species.*

Flexibility can be derived by distinguishing between *what* and *how*. Congress decides *what* the ESA should accomplish but should give flexibility to agencies and landowners in determining *how* to achieve it. Currently, the ESA allows flexibility, and numerous voluntary, creative partnerships have been formed between the FWS and farmers, ranchers, developers, and timber companies to protect listed species, wetlands, and other habitat (Chapter 6). Reauthorization of the ESA should support increased emphasis on flexibility in developing partnerships with private property owners.

3. *Landowners need more certainty with respect to implementation of the ESA.*

It is acknowledged that many ranchers and private property owners, both individual and corporate, are good stewards of their lands and would willingly cooperate with the ESA if there were more certainty about how the process will evolve. Landowners fear the financial and livelihood consequences of having an endangered species or designated critical habitat on their land. The FWS and NMFS should continue to explore official agreements that would both protect species and offer long-term certainty to landowners. The recently developed safe harbors approach, for example, assures landowners that if voluntary land management activities result in increased endangered species numbers beyond the existing numbers on that land, the landowner will not be subject to undue additional restrictions. Ideally, the ESA should encourage testing of private initiatives and dissemination of creative solutions that achieve the goals of the law while addressing landowners' concerns.

4. *Environmental goals of the ESA should be aligned with economic incentives.*

Evaluation of current implementation of the ESA raises the question of whether private property owners face undue burdens that become disincentives for conservation. Legislative changes related to the ESA should treat citizens as customers with legitimate concerns, and should facilitate development of incentives and removal of disincentives. *The ESA mandates conservation; it should also reward conservation.* When environmental goals are complemented by economic incentives, many of which may involve only modest public financing, we will likely have a more effective, fair, and workable law.

Consensus-based reports such as those emerging from the Keystone Center,[1] and analyses by groups like the Western Governors' Association[2] and Defenders of Wildlife,[3] provide useful points for discussing incentive-based policies. Financial incentives could include income tax credits or deductions for conservation expenses, or property tax credits for lands under permanent conservation easements. Other incentives could take the form of increased participation in decision making, increased availability of technical assistance, and increased flexibility in management plans. These are provided as examples only; much work is needed in exploring alternatives and developing consensus on efficient approaches.

The evaluation of all incentives should include consideration of what the costs are and who will pay. Efforts are needed to develop creative new and reliable funding sources to support collaborative efforts on private lands.

5. The ESA should encourage efficient use of resources through elimination of duplicative NEPA requirements and reduction of multiple agency oversight.

Private property owners may be contacted by more than one agency (federal, state, and/or local) regarding a listed species or the identification of critical habitat. This can result in landowner confusion and agency inefficiency. It is a worthwhile goal to reduce multiple agency oversight and eliminate duplicative regulatory requirements within the National Environmental Policy Act. The lead agency responsible for developing habitat conservation plans (under Section 10 of the ESA) with private property owners should be clearly identified, and should define a baseline that enables incremental consultation, allowing changes without reopening the entire process. A reauthorized ESA should establish when agency consultations under Section 7 should be conducted for approving, issuing, or modifying an incidental take permit. Agencies should increase support for personnel training in communication and collaboration on endangered species issues.

6. The ESA should recognize the differences in the scale of economic, cultural, and social impacts for large and small property owners and allow for implementation to be adjusted accordingly.

Private property interests include individual, tribal, and corporate owners. There is a difference in the scale of economic, cultural, and social impacts for very large and very small property owners, and in the financial and technical resources available for dealing with those impacts (Chapter 5). Agencies need to be responsive to the different objectives, needs, and goals of various owners.

7. Much more emphasis should be placed on proactive management to prevent the need for species to be listed under the ESA.

Many potential conflicts with private property owners can be reduced or eliminated through efforts to avoid the necessity of listing species under the ESA. Actions to prevent species decline, entered into voluntarily with private property owners, could reduce the number of species requiring ESA intervention. The IENR board strongly emphasizes the importance of trying to keep species off the endangered lists in the first place. Once a species is endangered, recovery is all the more difficult and costly. Further collaborative discussions are needed to identify adequate sources of funding for these innovations. One way to improve the act would be for the ESA to provide additional funding for information and administrative resources that encourage voluntary collaborative initiatives and local efforts.

8. Decisions regarding the protection of species and habitat conservation should be well grounded in sound social and natural science.

As emphasized in a recent National Research Council evaluation of science and the ESA,[4] sound science is an essential starting point throughout all processes called for in the act. Efforts to resolve conflicts between private property owners and the ESA would benefit from reliable information, but often information is unavailable or difficult to evaluate. For example, few, if any, thorough, objective studies of the effects of the ESA on private property owners have been published in the scientific literature.

Sound science is especially essential during the listing process. The current act states that listing must be based on the best scientific and commercial trade data available. Because of the complexity of these deliberations, decisions should be based on multidisciplinary, integrated scientific findings. Further, the ESA should allow the development of consistent and objective criteria for agencies to use when weighing scientific information in the listing process.

The federal government needs to renew efforts to assure that information given to private property owners is clear and comprehensive as to the biological and economic costs and benefits. Evaluating these costs and benefits is often difficult, and additional research is needed in the areas of land-use economics and how to value preservation of biodiversity.

CONCLUSION

Involvement of all stakeholders, provision for goal-based flexibility and certainty for landowners, and alignment of environmental goals with economic incentives could form the basis of innovative approaches to achieving the ESA's management objectives. Reduction of multiple agency oversight, recognition of the different scales of property ownership, and voluntary management to prevent the need to list species would also help diminish conflicts with landowners. All decisions should be grounded in sound science that is communicated as clearly as possible. We must all look at new, creative, bold ways to build bridges with the nation's property owners and provide incentives to them for protection of our natural resources.

The preceding recommendations regarding the Endangered Species Act as it applies to private property are the result of a consensus among the following members of the Institute for Environment and Natural Resources Board.

John Mack Carter	Roy L. Cline	William R. Corbin
Thomas Crocker	Brian R. Croft	Charles W. Duncan Jr.
Hank Fischer	Jim Geringer	William A. Gern
James C. Hageman	David L. Harrison	Stanley K. Hathaway
Erivan Haub	Helga Haub	John Hughes
Thomas C. Jensen	William Johnson	Albert K. Karnig
Donald M. Kendall	Forrest M. Kepler	William J. Kirby
Thomas A. Lockhart	Cynthia M. Lummis	Whitney MacMillan
Earl K. Madsen	Alan Maki	Robert M. McGee
Terry O'Connor	Richard L. Perrine	Edward Pollak
Terry P. Roark	G. Jon Roush	William Doyle Ruckelshaus
Alan K. Simpson	Peter K. Simpson	Polly T. Strife
Theodore Strong	Jane Metzler Sullivan	Mike Sullivan
Jack T. Turnell	Robert K. Turner	Thad A. Wolfe

NOTES

1   The Keystone Center, *Dialogue on Incentives for Private Landowners to Protect Endangered Species: Final Report* (Keystone, Colo., 1995).
2   Western Governors' Association, *Essential Elements of Amendments to the Endangered Species Act* (Denver, 1995).
3   H. Fischer and W. E. Hudson, *Building Economic Incentives into the Endangered Species Act* (Washington, D.C.: Defenders of Wildlife, 1994).
4   National Research Council, *Science and the Endangered Species Act* (Washington, D.C.: National Academy Press, 1995).

Contributors

Stanley H. Anderson is the leader of the Wyoming Cooperative Fish & Wildlife Research Unit and professor of zoology and physiology at the University of Wyoming, Laramie.

Michael J. Brennan is an attorney in the Jackson, Wyoming, office of Holland & Hart LLP. Michael also practices with the firm's Endangered Species Act working group.

Murray D. Feldman is an attorney in the Boise, Idaho, office of Holland & Hart LLP. He practices with the firm's Endangered Species Act working group.

Patricia Hayward is a zoology research associate in Laramie, Wyoming.

Jeffrey A. Lockwood is professor of plant, soil, and insect sciences at the University of Wyoming.

Jason Rylander is the former managing editor of the *Land Letter,* a publication of The Conservation Fund. He is currently enrolled in law school.

Jason F. Shogren is the Stroock Distinguished Professor of Natural Resource Conservation and Management and professor of economics at the University of Wyoming. In 1997, he served as the senior economist for environmental and natural resource policy on the President's Council of Economic Advisers.

John F. Turner is a third-generation Wyoming rancher and outfitter, past president of the Wyoming State Senate, former Director of the U.S. Fish and Wildlife Service, and the current President and Chief Operating Officer of the Conservation Fund in Washington, D.C.

Index

California Riparian Habitat Joint Venture, 129
Cameron County, Texas, 106–108
candidate species, 22–23
Cantrell, Mark, 102
case law, 3, 10
Central Valley, California, 125
chickadee, 128
Christy v. Hodel, 38, 39, 40
CITES, 12, 13, 15, 18
Clark County, Nevada, 57
Clark Fork Basin Committee, xiii
Clean Air Act, 10, 117
Clean Water Act, 110, 112
Clinton administration, 95, 99, 114
Coexistence Committee, 107–108
Colorado River basin, 56, 57
Commission on Old Growth Alternatives, xiii
common law, 10
Community Assistance Programs, 116
Community-based Recovery Planning, 85
compensation for taking of private property, 4, 6, 77, 80, 114–115
Comprehensive Environmental Response, Compensation, and Liability Act, 55
conservation agreements, 104–108
conservation banking, 122–123
Conservation Reserve Program, 98, 116, 118
constitutional takings. *See* regulatory takings
Constitution of the United States, 9–10, 13
consultation process, 17, 18, 27, 31–32, 41–42
contingent valuation method, 61–63
Convention for the Protection of Migratory Birds, 11
Convention on International Trade in Endangered Species of Wild Fauna and Flora, 12, 13, 15, 18
Convention on Natural Protection and Wildlife Preservation in the Western Hemisphere, 11, 15, 18

Convention with the Union of Soviet Socialist Republics on the Conservation of Migratory Birds and Their Environment, 13
costs of endangered species, 1, 54–58
critical habitat, 28, 77; designation of, 16, 20–21, 27; economic impact of designating, 54, 56–57; pending legislation for, 110–111

delisting of species, 20, 52
Department of Agriculture, 118
Department of Commerce, 19–20, 21, 27
Department of the Interior, 19–20, 21, 27, 38, 74, 112, 118
de Tocqueville, Alexis, 93–94
development rights, 14, 117, 121–122
Dolan v. City of Tigard, 35, 36, 37–38, 39, 42–43
Draft Safe Harbor Policy, 104
Ducks Unlimited, 14
Dwyer, William, 28

easements, 14, 141
Ecological Society of America ad hoc committee, 53
ecosystems, 28, 31, 53, 74–75, 109
endangered species, 2, 57; benefits of, 48–49, 58–64, 81; defined, 26–27; listing of, 12, 19–20; on private property, 94; prohibited acts against, 18; risk to, 1, 3; spending on, 57–58; as symptoms, 75–76. *See also* candidate species; threatened species
Endangered Species Act: authority of, 97; benefits of, 1, 58–64; biological effectiveness of, 49–53, 64; connectedness scale of, 74–76, 78, 85; costs of, 1, 4–5, 54–58; economic criteria in, 54; evolution of, 9–15; focus of, 25–26; and habitat conservation, 26, 29–32; improving implementation of, 5; 1988 amendments of, 22; perspectives of, 76–81; prohibited acts under, 18; proposed legislation,

150

Index

habitat: acquisition of, 12, 13–15, 16;
    conservation, 26, 29–32, 53, 109–
    110; conservation plans, 4, 82–83,
    84, 85, 98–100, 110; intentional
    destruction of, 82; modification, 26,
    27, 32–34, 40–41; regulations con-
    cerning, 11, 12; value of, 48–49. *See
    also* critical habitat
Habitat Transaction Method, 122
harm, 32–34, 109
Hawaii, 32
Hayden, Mike, 110
hermit thrush, 128
Holtrop, Joel, 106
Huachuca water umbel, 128
Hutchison, Kay Bailey, 110
hypothetical market, 61

Idaho, 31, 29, 30
incentives for conservation on private
    land, 4–6, 83, 98, 108, 111, 115–
    123; and environmental goals of
    Endangered Species Act, 140–141
incidental take, 5, 82–83, 104; defined,
    28; permits, 4, 18, 41–42, 98, 112.
    See also taking of wildlife
Interagency Grizzly Bear Committee,
    105
International Association of Fish and
    Wildlife Agencies, 130
International Convention for the High
    Seas Fisheries of the North Pacific
    Ocean, 15
International Convention for the North-
    west Atlantic Fisheries, 15
international cooperation, 73
International Paper Company, 99

Jamison Strategy, 30
Jefferson, Thomas, 131
jeopardy opinion, 17, 27, 105

Kansas, 127
Kentucky, 38
Keystone Center, 117, 120–121, 131,
    138
Kirtland's warbler, 128

Lacey Act, 11
land: acquisition of for wildlife, 13–15;
    ethic, 86, 93–94, 124–125, 132;
    exchanges, 120–121
landowners. *See* private property owners
Lane County Audubon Society v. Jamison, 30
least Bell's vireo, 129
Leopold, Aldo, 81, 86, 113, 133
listed species. *See* endangered species;
    threatened species
listing of species, 12, 13, 19–20, 77,
    139–140; avoiding, 142
Llano Seco Ranch, California, 125
Louisiana, 55
Louisiana Forestry Association, 96
Loveladies Harbor, Inc. v. United States,
    39–40, 43
Lucas v. South Carolina Coastal Council,
    35, 36–37, 39, 40

Mad Island Marsh, Texas, 125
marbled murrelet, 41
Marbled Murrelet v. Babbitt, 34
marginal species, 60
markets, 3, 48–49; hypothetical, 61
Massachusetts, 40
Memorandum of Understanding, 83
Mexico, 124
Michigan, 128
Migratory Bird Hunting Stamp Act
    (1934), 14
migratory birds, 11, 12, 13; acquisition
    of refuges for, 14
Migratory Bird Treaty Act (1918), 14
Mississippi, 100
mitigation banking, 122, 123
mitigation fees, 83–84
Montana, 29, 105–106
Morrill v. Lujan, 33
Mount Graham red squirrel, 17
multiple agency oversight, 141
multispecies conservation, 99–100. *See
    also* biodiversity

Nashville warbler, 128
National Biological Diversity Reserve
    Lands, 111